WELLINGTON'S PENINSULAR VICTORIES

MICHAEL GLOVER

THE AUTHOR

Michael Glover was educated at Oundle and St John's College, Cambridge where he read history. During the Second World War he served in Tunisia and Italy until taken prisoner commanding a company of Sherwood Foresters with orders to 'Cross the Rubicon'. After the war, he served in the Territorial Army and worked for the British Council until 1970 when he withdrew to the Cotswolds to devote himself to writing military history. He had written over twenty books when he died in 1990.

WELLINGTON'S PENINSULAR VICTORIES

MICHAEL GLOVER

THE WINDRUSH PRESS · GLOUCESTERSHIRE

For Daphne

First published in Great Britain by
B.T. Batsford Ltd, 1963
Reprinted by The Windrush Press, 1996
Little Window, High Street,
Moreton-in-Marsh
Gloucestershire GL56 0LL
Telephone: 01608 652012
Fax: 01608 652125

British Library Cataloguing in Publication Data
A catalogue record for this book is available from the British Library

ISBN 0 900624 01 X

Typeset by Archetype, Stow-on-the-Wold
Printed and bound in Great Britain by Bell & Bain Ltd., Glasgow

The front cover shows a detail from a painting of the Battle of Vitoria, 21 June 1813, by
courtesy of Peter Newark's Military Pictures

Contents

Preface

For a work which avowedly deals with battles, Wellington's campaigns in Portugal, Spain and the South of France present the author with an embarrassingly large number of subjects. I have followed the plan of dealing with one of the actions which Wellington fought against each of his principal opponents, Masséna (1810–11), Marmont 1811–12), King Joseph (1812–13) and Soult (1813–14).

Shortage of space has also prevented me from indulging myself in many of the favourite topics of Peninsular historians, such as whether Wellington was a better general than (a) Marlborough or (b) Napoleon, and whether the British Army was held together by the constant use of the cat-o'-nine-tails. I have strong views on all these subjects, but this does not seem to be the place to deploy them.

Wherever possible I have tried to use the words of participants. There are obvious pitfalls in this approach but they seem to me to be worth risking. In cases where there is conflicting evidence or insufficient evidence I have fallen back on what the late Lt.-Col. A. H. Burne described as 'inherent military probability'.

I must acknowledge, as must every Peninsular historian, my debt of gratitude to Sir William Napier, Sir John Fortescue and Sir Charles Oman. Without their scholarship and industry a work such as this could not be written in less than a lifetime.

My thanks are also due to Brigadier J. Stephenson and the library staff of the Royal United Service Institution, to Miss Seymour Whinyates, Mr. Bernard Adams, Mr. Oliver Warner and Mr. John Naylor. Most of all I am indebted to my wife and daughter for their advice and encouragement.

Illustrations

'March of Baggage following the Army, 16th May 1811' from an aquatint by C. Turner after a watercolour drawing by Major T. St. Clair
by courtesy of the Trustees of the British Museum

'A halt in the Pyrenees, July 1813 'from an aquatint by J.C. Stadler after a drawing by W. Heath

The Battle of Salamanca, 22nd July 1813 from an engraving by J. Clark and M. Dubourg after a drawing by W. Heath
by courtesy of the Trustees of the British Museum

The Battle of the Bidassoa, 9th October 1813 from an engraving by D. Havell after a drawing by W. Heath
by courtesy of the Trustees of the British Museum

The Battle of the Nivelle, 10th November 1813 from an engraving by T. Sutherland after a drawing by W. Heath
by courtesy of the Trustees of the British Museum

'Attack on the road to Bayonne' The Battle of the Nive from an engraving by T. Sutherland after a drawing by W. Heath
by courtesy of the Trustees of the British Museum

MAPS AND PLANS IN THE TEXT

Prologue

Sir Arthur Wellesley

On 30th June 1808, Lord Castlereagh, Secretary of State for War, wrote to his colleague Sir Arthur Wellesley, Chief Secretary for Ireland, 'The occupation of Spain and Portugal by the troops of France, and the entire usurpation of their respective governments by that power, has determined his Majesty to direct a corps of his troops to be prepared for service, to be employed under your orders, in counteracting the designs of the enemy, and in affording to the Spanish and Portuguese nations every possible aid in throwing off the yoke of France.' The aim of the expedition was to be, 'the final and absolute evacuation of the Peninsula by the troops of France'. The force allocated to Wellesley for this purpose consisted of 13,500 men.

In November 1807 a French corps of 20,000 men under General Junot had occupied Portugal without encountering any resistance, although they had suffered terribly from the hardships of the march since Napoleon had insisted on their advancing along the line of the Tagus, a route that was all but impassable. Their declared aim was to close the harbours of Portugal to British trade. Junot had had every co-operation from the Spanish authorities and Spanish troops formed part of the army of occupation.

Hardly was Portugal subdued than the Emperor turned his attention to his ally. By the spring French troops occupied a triangle of Spain with its base on the Pyrenees and its apex at Madrid. The next step was to force the abdication of the King, to make the Prince of the Asturias renounce his rights of succession and to appoint Joseph Bonaparte to the vacant throne. This was too much for the Spanish people, little as they had admired their own dynasty. On 2nd May 1808 a minor but significant riot broke out in Madrid and was suppressed with much bloodshed by the French. By the end of the month all the outlying provinces had declared war on France and by the first week of June Asturian delegates were in London asking for British arms and money. Castilian troops were in action against the French on 12th June at Cabezon near Valladolid and although they were defeated, French troops were heavily repulsed when they tried to storm Saragossa and Valencia. The revolt spread to northern Portugal.

Wellesley sailed from Cork on 12th July. While he was still at sea the Spaniards won their greatest victory of the war. Twenty thousand French troops were surrounded and forced to surrender at Baylen. It was the heaviest French defeat for more than a decade and caused King Joseph to evacuate his new capital.

The British force landed at Mondego Bay on 1st August. The beach had been secured by Portuguese patriots and the sand was 'hot enough almost to have dressed a beefsteak'. Wellesley was greeted on landing by the news that the Government had decided to expand his corps to a strength of 40,000 men and that he was to be superseded in command by no fewer than three senior officers. Fortunately none of them arrived before he had time to deal decisively with Junot's army.

The small army which landed in Portugal was not untypical of the kind of force which the British government had, for the past 16 years, been despatching to widely scattered and usually inhospitable coasts in the hope of doing some harm to the apparently invincible French. The majority of these expeditions had ended in well-merited disaster. Wellesley's force consisted of thirteen and a half battalions of excellent infantry, the equal of any in Europe but there was little or nothing to support it. There were 394 light dragoons who had 180 horses between them. Three batteries of artillery had no horses at all, and could not be moved from the beach until Portuguese horses had been requisitioned. The supply services were particularly sketchy. Transport and supply were the responsibility of the Treasury who contributed money and a number of civilian officials, 'commissaries', whose function it was to hire the necessary carts and draught animals and to arrange for the purchase of food and fodder. This system had, occasionally, worked fairly well in the Low Countries. In Portugal, it bore little relation to the situation in the country and no previous arrangements had been made since, as Castlereagh informed Wellesley, 'the great delay and expense that would attend embarking and sending . . . all those means which would be requisite to render the army completely mobile on landing, has determined his Majesty's Government to trust in great measure, to the resources of the country for their supplies.' Fortunately Wellesley had been able to use his political position in Ireland to include in the expedition two companies of the Royal Irish Corps of Waggoners whose few springed carts were useful for transporting wounded.

It was eight days before the army could leave the beach. By that time it had been possible to acquire 500 mules, 300 bullocks and 60 more dragoon horses. Nevertheless one of the artillery batteries had to be left behind for want of draught animals.

Junot had had ample warning of the British landing and sent 4,000 men under General Delaborde to delay them while the rest of his army could be concentrated. The first clash, a very minor affair, occurred at Obidos on 15th August, and two days later Wellesley's centre, contrary to his intentions, frontally attacked Delaborde's force at Roliça. The French lost 600 men and three guns, the British 474. Both actions were without tactical significance but they showed to those who would see that the British infantry had acquired a new virtue – initiative. For centuries the outstanding attribute of the British foot-soldier had been his disciplined steadiness in battle, the kind of dogged courage which had shown to such advantage at Hastings, Agincourt, Blenheim, Fontenoy and Minden. Their wars in America had shown that this was not enough. From the humiliations of the American War of Independence had come a new school of thought which was not satisfied with an army of savagely disciplined automata but trained the soldier to think for himself and to rely on himself and his comrades. Leadership became an art to be cultivated and discipline a matter of pride and consent. The roots of this school lay in the teachings of Wolfe and Amherst but realisation was brought about by John Moore when he trained his brigade at Shorncliffe in 1803.

The new spirit had by no means spread throughout the army by 1808, but the regiments which Moore had indoctrinated, the 43rd, the 52nd and the 95th Rifles supplied a leaven for the rest of the force. 'In them', Moore had written, 'it is evident that not only the officers, but that every individual soldier knows perfectly what he has to do; the discipline is carried out without severity; the officers are attached to the men, the men to the officers. The men find that pains are taken to keep them from doing wrong, that allowances are made for trivial faults, and that they are not punished for serious crimes until advice and every other means have been resorted to in vain.' This was very different from the old school of discipline in which, 'if a man coughed in the ranks, he was punished; if the sling of the firelock for an instant left his shoulder when it should not, he was punished; and if he moved his knapsack when standing at ease, he was punished'.

On 21st August, Junot, who had collected together 11,000 infantry, 2,000 cavalry and 23 guns attacked Wellesley at Vimeiro where he had drawn up his army to cover the disembarkation of two brigades of reinforcements, bringing his force up to 17,000 men. Junot, like Napoleon and most of his generals, judged British military performance on memories of their expeditions to the Netherlands in the Revolutionary war. Being convinced that a sharp push would send Wellesley scuttling back to the ships, the main French attack was made frontally, in column. It was beaten back three times with heavy loss. The arrival, as the French were finally repulsed, of one of the generals designated to supersede

Wellesley meant that there could be no pursuit and when, the following day, the most senior of all landed, the army was reduced to complete immobility, but the French asked for a convention and were allowed to evacuate Portugal on generous terms. Wellesley returned to England and with his two seniors faced a court of inquiry forced on the Government by the fury of George III and his people who reckoned that the fruits of Vimeiro had been thrown away by timidity and incompetence.

Vimeiro was a most important battle. Not only did it result in the liberation of Portugal, but, although the French refused to learn the lesson, it showed that the methods by which the armies of Revolutionary and Imperial France had conquered the armies of monarchist Europe would not do against a well-led British army. Although the *Ordounance* of 1791, the basic tactical document of the French army, had enjoined a battle-formation in three ranks the French commanders had found that heavy masses of men in column, provided that they were shrouded in a dense cloud of skirmishers and heavily supported by artillery, could break their way through an enemy line like a battering-ram. Against armies which were not altogether steady this theory worked magnificently but against the British, who refused to be frightened by an imposing mass of shouting troops advancing against them at the double, it was a total failure. The column wasted fire-power for only the men in the front two ranks could use their muskets. The British generals, also disregarding their instructions, reduced their line of battle to two deep, thus permitting every weapon to be brought to bear. Therefore, if the British could be drawn up where the ground did not expose them overmuch to the French artillery, and having trained skirmishers as competent and as numerous as the French, their traditional steadiness could be counted on to keep them to their posts until the time came for them, on the order being given, to blow away the heads of the French columns with a series of terrible volleys. Wellesley had learned this simple truth before he sailed for Portugal. Napoleon had still to learn it at Waterloo.

As soon as Wellesley had been absolved from all blame by the court of inquiry he was sent back to command the army in Portugal. During his absence the situation had greatly changed. Determined to avenge the humiliation of Baylen, Napoleon marched into Spain at the head of a quarter of a million veterans of the *Grande Armée*. Cutting through the Spanish resistance, the Emperor reached Madrid on 3rd December, planning, after a necessary pause, to go on to Lisbon. Great was his surprise when he learned, little more than a fortnight after reaching Madrid, that Sir John Moore with 30,000 men from the British army in Portugal was to his north at Sahagun and threatening his communications with France.

Abandoning his westward drive, Napoleon with the corps of Soult and Ney, hurried off to deal with the presumptuous Moore. As soon as it was clear that the British could not be cut off from the sea, Napoleon handed over command to Soult and returned to Paris. Moore made good his escape and, turning to await the arrival of the fleet, inflicted a sharp defeat on his pursuers at Coruña.

The details of Moore's generalship have been the subject of much controversy. There can be no doubt of his achievement. The entire French plan for the subjugation of the Peninsula was dislocated; their striking-force was drawn away into an inhospitable *cul-de-sac* in the mountains of Galicia, and their chance of retaking Lisbon was gone for ever.

While Moore had been making his raid into Spain, a force of 10,000 British troops had remained in Portugal under Sir John Cradock, a timorous officer. For some months his only plan had been to take up a defensive position in rear of Lisbon and to make careful preparations for embarking the army. At the end of March, Soult, whose orders from the Emperor called on him to march on Lisbon from Coruña by way of Vigo, reached Oporto with an army in the last stages of exhaustion. He was two months behind his Imperial schedule, but he had no option but to give his troops a prolonged rest. Wellesley returned to the Portuguese capital on 22nd April with a firm mandate as Commander-in-Chief of the British and Portuguese armies. He spent a week in Lisbon trying to impose some kind of order on the commissariat, and then, having sent small Anglo-Portuguese forces to watch the eastern frontier, marched north 'to beat or cripple Soult'. He had 18,000 men, one-ninth of them Portuguese.

Soult had 13,000 men in Oporto and received from his cavalry and from other sources ample warning of the allied approach. He had made up his mind to retreat into Spain but felt that, with the great width of the Douro between him and Wellesley, there could be no reason to leave hurriedly. He had all the river-boats brought over to the north bank, destroyed his bridge of boats and posted strong guards on the town waterfront and between the town and the sea, for he feared that the Royal Navy might land troops in his rear. He spent the night of 11/12th May at his desk making his dispositions and retired to his bed as dawn broke. At that moment a staff officer was reporting to Wellesley that he had found a skiff on the south bank and that with it and the aid of some Portuguese peasants he had brought to the south bank three wine-barges. 'Let the men cross', said Sir Arthur.

An hour later half the Buffs were across and established in a walled seminary on the river-bank. It was only then that the French discovered their presence. Three battalions attacked the seminary but were swept away by the fire of 18 guns firing onto their flank from the heights across the Douro. By the time that a further French attack could be mounted two more British battalions had been ferried across and the attack failed. Determined to drive the British away, Soult withdrew his battalions from the town quay. Immediately the inhabitants crossed the river in every available craft and filling them with troops returned to the north bank. Two British brigades stormed through the town to find the French making off in disorder towards Spain. Wellesley's men suffered 123 casualties.

Soult was not at the end of his troubles. He found the road to Spain blocked by an Anglo-Portuguese force. With Wellesley at his heels there was no time to settle down to driving this force from a strong position. Abandoning their artillery, their reserve ammunition and the military chest containing £50,000, the French took a goat-track over the Serra do Santa Catalina, reaching Orense on 19th May having suffered 4,000 casualties since Wellesley moved against them 10 days earlier.

Wellesley fought many brilliant and successful actions against the French, but he never again did anything so risky as when he threw 370 men of the Buffs across the broad Douro in the face of 13,000 Frenchmen. The French continued to regard him as a cautious commander.

Having liberated Portugal for the second time, Wellesley turned his attention to the danger that threatened the country on its eastern frontier. Marshal Victor, Duke of Belluno, with 20,000 men, was lying at Merida, to the east of Badajoz. His orders were to move on Lisbon as soon as he heard that Soult was marching south from Oporto. No word of Soult had reached him for more than four months and he devoted such energy as he could spare from finding food for his men, to watching the slight covering force that Wellesley had sent in his direction and, more especially, a large and ramshackle Spanish army, under General Cuesta, the Captain-General of Estremadura, which was manœuvring somewhat aimlessly to his south.

Determined to try to co-operate with the Spanish armies as he had been ordered to do, Wellesley arranged to make a joint move towards Madrid with Cuesta. The arrangements were hard to make as the Spaniard, Wellesley complained, was 'obstinate as any gentleman at the head of an army ought to be', but eventually the combined armies were concentrated at Talavera.

Here on 27th and 28th July they were attacked by 50,000 Frenchmen, the combined corps of King Joseph, Victor and Sébastiani. The whole brunt of the attack fell on the 20,000 British and German troops, while the 33,000 Spaniards were contained for most of the day by 2,000 French dragoons.

The first French attack, during the night of 27th July surprised some outposts, and almost captured Rowland Hill, the commander of the Second Division, who hearing firing in the night rode up to the spot on the assumption that 'it was the old Buffs, as usual, making some blunder'. The situation was restored by 'a dashing charge in open column' by the 29th. A renewed attack on the following morning in greater strength met with no more success. The crisis of the battle came when, during the afternoon, the French threw 14,000 infantry against the British line. In the centre 14,000 men advanced against the eight battalions of the First Division. For more than an hour they had stood on the most exposed part of the front with no cover of any kind, suffering terribly from a heavy artillery preparation before two French divisions advanced against them. 'General Sherbroke had cautioned his men to use the bayonet, and when the enemy came within about fifty yards of the Guards they advanced to meet them, but on their attempting to close the enemy with a charge, they broke and fled . . . but the impetuosity of the Guards led to endangering the day. The flying enemy led them on till they opened a battery on their flank, which occasioned so heavy a loss, that the ranks could not be formed after the disorder of pursuit, and on being ordered to resume their ground, led to confusion. The enemy instantly rallied and followed them, and were so confident of victory, that their officers were heard to exclaim, "*Allons, mes enfants, ils sont tous nos prisonniers*".' Since the whole of the First Division had followed the example of the Guards and had been similarly driven back, the moment was critical as more than a thousand yards of the British centre was wide open. Wellesley was equal to the situation. He called forward his reserve brigade and sent down a single battalion from his left and with this slight force held back the French onslaught long enough for the First Division to reform.

The French did not attack again. The battle had cost them more than 7,000 men and news had reached them that another Spanish army was moving against their rear. They fell back, slowly and reluctantly. Wellesley could not, and Cuesta would not pursue. More than a quarter of the British army were casualties and the troops who had fought the battle on half-rations, were reduced to one-third-rations on the day following. Four thousand wounded were in need of attention and even those who were unhurt were almost too exhausted to undertake the work of burying the dead and carrying the wounded to improvised hospitals in Talavera. It was fortunate that on the morning after the battle, Robert Crauford with three battalions of the Light Brigade arrived to take over the outposts and to assist in 'collecting the dead bodies and putting them into large heaps with faggots and burning them'. Even these could scarcely be counted as fresh troops. In their eagerness to arrive in time for the battle they had marched 42 miles in 26 hours under the burning heat of the Spanish summer.

For six days after the battle, the British stayed on the ground they had held. Rations became shorter every day. Desperately Wellesley tried to hold the Spanish authorities to their promises of food and urged them to let him have transport for his mass of wounded. Nothing was forthcoming. While this dilemma was still unresolved a new danger arose in the rear. On 3rd August Wellesley learned from a captured letter that Soult had evacuated the whole north-western corner of Spain, and gathering up troops from the Asturias and Leon as he came, was marching on the British communications with Portugal with 50,000 men. As this news reached Wellesley, British and French cavalry were in action at Naval Moral 35 miles to the west of Talavera and the main body of Soult's infantry had reached Palencia. There was no time to be lost. Leaving the wounded in the care of Cuesta, who abandoned them, the British army marched westward on the south bank of the Tagus. A remarkable cross-country march by the Light Brigade, 'scrambling over the mountains' on a diet of 'boiled wheat and dried peas, without bread, salt or meat', secured the vital bridge at Almaraz, the only crossing by which Soult could have reached the army's escape route. By the end of the month the whole army was safely back on the Portuguese frontier, around Badajoz.

This was Wellesley's first and last attempt to co-operate with large Spanish forces not under his own command. It had not been a success and might well have been a disastrous failure. The British retreat to Portugal was regarded by the Spaniards as desertion, but Wellesley would not be deterred. 'I lament as much as any man can the necessity of separating from the Spaniards', he wrote on 1st September, 'but I was compelled to go, and I believe there was not an officer in the army who did not think I stayed too long . . . . The fault I committed consisted in trusting at all to the Spaniards, who I have since found were entirely unworthy of confidence'.

PART ONE

Wellington and Masséna

1

The 'Cautious System'

The year 1810 was to be the turning-point in the Peninsular War. 1809 had been an interregnum. For the whole campaigning season, the main strength of the French army had been committed to war with Austria. In May Napoleon had been held to a draw at Aspern and Essling and it was not until the Austrians had been crushed at Wagram in July that he was again able to turn his attention to the problems of Spain and Portugal. He set about strengthening his armies there and by the New Year 360,000 French troops were either in Spain or were concentrating at Bayonne ready to cross the Pyrenees.

While Napoleon's first priority was to rid the Peninsula of the British army, he could not employ all these men for the purpose. The attempt to subdue Aragon and Catalonia, an attempt which never succeeded in six years of war, needed 78,000 men. Fourteen thousand were required to hold Madrid and the surrounding country. Soult was concentrating 60,000 to invade Andalusia and more than 60,000 men were in north-eastern Spain holding open the supply routes from Bayonne to Madrid and Salamanca.

The Andalusian campaign was not a success. The province was overrun with the greatest of ease but Soult's victorious army was halted in front of the isthmus which joins Cadiz to the mainland. There they maintained some kind of a siege until the late summer of 1812. In consequence a large French army had always to be kept in this corner of Spain which only in the most desperate emergency could raise a field force of even 20,000 men for use against the British.

Despite all these deductions a very large force was available to deal with the British; and there can have been few in France who entertained doubts about its adequacy for the task. Not only was the French army great in numbers. It had for many years shown itself to be the finest in Europe and, not without reason, believed itself to be invincible. The soldiers were brave, determined, hardy and self-reliant. The officers were chosen by merit and closely associated with their men. The commanders, although loth to co-operate with each other without the dominating presence of the Emperor, were the finest vintage of generals that any country has ever produced.

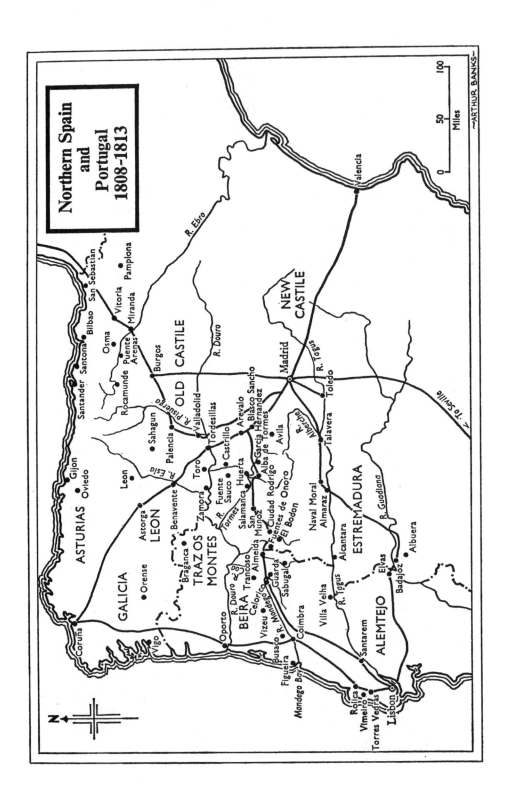

Northern Spain
and
Portugal
1808–1813

~ARTHUR BANKS~

100

50

0

Miles

R. Ebro

San Sebastian
Pamplona
Bilbao
Vitoria
Santander
Santona
Miranda
Osma
Puente
Arenas
Rocamunde
Burgos
R. Pisuerga
R. Douro
OLD CASTILE
NEW CASTILE
Valladolid
Arevalo
Tordesillas
Blasco Sancho
Sahagun
Castrillo
Garcia Hernandez
Palencia
Huerta
Alba de Tormes
Toro
Leon
Fuente
Sauco
Avila
Salamanca
San
Muñoz
R. Esla
R. Tormes
Ciudad Rodrigo
El Bodon
Fuentes de Onoro
Madrid
R. Tagus
Toledo
Talavera
R. Alberche
Naval Moral
Almaraz
Gijon
Oviedo
ASTURIAS
Benavente
LEON
Astorga
Zamora
TRAZOS
MONTES
Braganca
Orense
GALICIA
Alcantara
ESTREMADURA
R. Tagus
R. Guadiana
Albuera
Coruña
Vigo
R. Douro
Trancoso
Almeida
BEIRA
Vizeu
Celorico
Guarda
Sabugal
Villa Velha
Elvas
Badajoz
Oporto
R. Mondego
Coimbra
ALEMTEJO
Busaco
Santarem
Figueira
Mondego Bay
Roliça
Vimeiro
Torres Vedras
Lisbon

To Seville

Valencia

N

With all its virtues, the French army carried the seed of its own destruction. Its supply system was quite unsuitable for the kind of war that it had to fight in the Peninsula. Napoleon's armies, to the great relief of the Imperial Treasury, were expected to maintain themselves in the districts in which they fought. It was a system that had worked well in the fertile lands of Lombardy, and the Danube basin, but it was bound to fail in the barren reaches of Spain and Portugal. In countries where the harvest was barely sufficient to support the population, it was impossible to maintain thousands of foreign soldiers. Hence the French armies in Spain had always to be on the move, and no concentration could last more than a few weeks before hunger enforced dispersion. Moreover, the ruthless methods of requisition which were needed to obtain even the bare necessities, earned for the French the lethal enmity of the peasantry.

To oppose this huge French army, the British commander, who was created Viscount Wellington of Talavera in the early autumn of 1809, could put in the field rather more than 26,000 British troops. There were, in addition, about 10,000 sick, some of them battle casualties, but the majority victims of the 'Guadiana fever' which had plagued the army after its retreat from Talavera. Despite its recent victories it was not a very strong army. Since the bulk of the troops which had landed in 1808 had gone with Moore to Coruña and, except for the Light Brigade, had been sent on their return on the abortive expedition to Walcheren, the army in Portugal was largely composed of second battalions. These, intended as feeding-units for their seniors, were seldom of the highest quality. 'There are really many in the army', wrote Wellington, 'that are quite unfit for service in respect of composition and discipline . . . the non-comissioned officers . . . are very bad; and I am sorry to add that the subaltern officers are not of the best description'. The few remaining battalions of the force which had landed with Wellesley in 1808 were now shadows of their former selves, as for example the 29th, which had landed in Mondego Bay 806 strong and had suffered almost 400 casualties in its four actions at Roliça, Vimeiro, Oporto and Talavera.

The greatest curse in the army was despondency, which in its turn increased the apprehensions of Perceval's tottering government in London. 'All the officers in the army', wrote the Secretary of State for War, 'whether they had served in the Peninsula or not, entertained the most despondent view as to the result of the war in that country. Not one officer, as far as I recollect, expressed . . . any confidence as to probable success, and not a mail arrived from Lisbon which did not bring letters . . . from officers of rank and situation in the army avowing their opinions as to the probability and even necessity of a speedy evacuation of the country'. Even General Hill, the most steadfast of all Wellington's lieutenants, wrote that 'to my mind the cause is *hopeless*' and was 'in daily expectation of a move towards England' with which course in view he bought four sheep from his landlord in Estremadura, 'to improve the Shropshire breed'. Wellington alone was confident. 'I am positively in no scrape; and if this country can be saved, we shall save it.'

It was inevitable that the task of saving Portugal must for the most part fall on the infantry. Britain was strong in cavalry, but the Government finding horsemen invaluable for quelling civil commotion, doled out to Wellington no more than three light and three heavy regiments. The provision of field artillery was barely adequate, the first two troops of Horse Artillery had arrived just too late for Talavera, and there was no siege artillery of any kind. The supply of Engineers was particularly inadequate, there being a total of 46 all ranks. As for the commissariat, Wellington wrote in despair, 'the existence of the army depends on it, and yet the people who manage it are incapable of managing anything out of a counting-house'.

About a tenth of the British strength in Portugal consisted of Germans enlisted in the British army. For the most part they consisted of a contingent of the King's German Legion, the successor body to George III's Hanoverian army, which in 1810 contributed four battalions, two field-batteries and a magnificent regiment of hussars to Wellington's strength. Also largely from Germany were the Riflemen of the 5th Battalion of the 60th Regiment, whose record in the war stands comparison with any in the army.

To compensate for his lack of British numbers, Wellington had to rely on Portuguese troops. At the beginning of the war the Portuguese army had been about as useless a body of men as was ever assembled. Fortunately the authorities, in 1809, had asked the British government to loan them a British general to train and under Wellington, to command their army. By an inspired choice William Carr Beresford, a very junior lieutenant-general, was appointed to this post. Although a field commander of only moderate ability, he was an organiser of genius. He had need to be. As one of his British staff wrote, 'The Portuguese soldier is naturally indolent. He falls with the greatest facility into slouching and slovenly habits, unless he is constantly roused and forced to exert himself. But many a Portuguese officer, if not constantly spurred and urged to do his duty, is at least as indolent as his men.'

Armed with full powers and helped by a cadre of British officers and N.C.O.s, Beresford beat the Portuguese army into shape. It was able to put in the field 24 regiments of infantry, each of two battalions and six, later twelve, battalions of *caçadores* (riflemen), beside seven field-batteries and a few dragoon regiments. By the time that he had finished with them they were, in the opinion of one British staff officer, 'Excellent troops equal to contend with the French infantry; under *ordinary circumstances* acting with the bravery of their island allies'.

As the Portuguese troops completed their training, Wellington was able, by the spring of 1810 to form them into divisions with his British and German soldiers. At first only two divisions conformed to what was to become the standard Anglo–Portuguese division, the Third, under Thomas Picton and the Fourth under Lowry Cole. These both consisted of two British brigades and one Portuguese. To these were attached a company of Riflemen from the 60th (the Portuguese brigades each had a battalion of *caçadores*) and a field-battery. Three other divisions were created at this time, the First (Sir Brent Spencer) and the Second (Rowland Hill) both consisted wholly of British troops, the First containing a brigade of the King's German Legion while the Second, which was usually employed on detached duty, had permanently attached to it a Portuguese division of two brigades. The other formation created at this time was the Light Division under Robert Craufurd. This was formed on the basis of the Light Brigade, the heirs to Moore's training, and was unique in that Portuguese troops were brigaded with British. Each of its two brigades originally consisted of one British Light Infantry battalion, one *caçadores* battalion and half (four companies) of the 1st Battalion 95th Rifles.

Little help could be looked for from the Spanish armies. Their governments and high commands were torn by provincial pride and personal jealousies and their military thought reverted constantly to the kind of concentric movement which, contrary to all probability, had won them the battle of Baylen. The plan never worked again and the Spanish generals earned a series of well-merited defeats. Nevertheless, as Hill remarked, 'their inveteracy towards the French is so great that they are formidable'. As long as the Spanish commanders could be persuaded to avoid general actions in open country, the mere existence of their armies lurking in the less accessible sierras forced the French to keep large forces available to counter their threats. Even more formidable were the *guerrilleros* who plagued the French lines of communication, tied down thousands of French troops and regularly provided Wellington with rich hauls of captured orders and despatches.

In the long run the issue of the war depended on Wellington. In May 1810 he was 41 and had been in the army since he was 17. Aided by potent influence and sufficient means to operate the system of purchase of commissions and promotion to his best advantage, his rise had been rapid. At 24 he was a lieutenant-colonel, having on his way, served, at least on paper, in seven regiments. In this rank he served in the Duke of York's campaign in the Low Countries in 1794–5 and learned 'what one ought not to do'. It was in India that he made his reputation. Here again influence was on his side, for although he arrived in Calcutta in 1797 no more than a brevet-colonel, the fact that his elder brother was Governor-General ensured that he received important and independent commands in the campaigns against Tippoo Sahib and the Mahrattas. At Assaye and Argaum he won two overwhelming victories which showed that he was more than worthy of the position that money and influence had gained for him. He showed also a mastery of logistics which was to stand him in good stead in the Peninsula.

Before landing in Portugal he had put his finger accurately on the great weakness of the French position. 'Buonaparte cannot carry on his operations in Spain, excepting by means of large armies; and I doubt much whether the country will afford subsistence for a large army, or if he will be able to supply his magazines from France, the roads being so bad and the communications so difficult.' With the experience of the campaigns of 1808 and 1809 behind him he was reinforced in his view. 'My opinion is, that as long as we shall remain in a state of activity in Portugal, the contest must continue in Spain; that the French are most desirous that we should withdraw from the country, but know that they must employ a very large force indeed in the operations which will render it necessary for us to go away; and I doubt whether they can bring that force to bear upon Portugal without abandoning other objects, and exposing their whole fabric in Spain to great risk. If they should be able to invade it, and should not succeed in obliging us to evacuate the country, they will be in a very dangerous position.'

It was possible to assess with a fair degree of certainty the route by which the French would advance for their third attempt to subdue Portugal. Only two roads were feasible for the movement of large armies. To the north, there was the *camino real* from Salamanca which crossed the frontier at Ciudad Rodrigo, and to the south the Madrid road which was dominated at the border by Badajoz. The latter was superficially more attractive since it ran through open, rolling country which would give scope for the powerful French cavalry, but there was one overriding drawback. The road never reached Lisbon. Instead it ended abruptly on the heights of Almada, within sight and heavy cannon-shot of the capital, but separated from it by the estuary of the Tagus, an estuary dominated by the Royal Navy, the one British force that no French general could hope to defeat. By this southern road might come a dangerous diversion and to cover it Wellington detached Rowland Hill, with a corps consisting of the Second Division, its attendant Portuguese formation and two British and two Portuguese regiments, a total of some 12,000 men.

The bulk of the army, four divisions, an independent Portuguese brigade and the remainder of the cavalry were left available to bar the road from Ciudad Rodrigo.

Something more than the Anglo-Portuguese army was needed to stop a French army that was likely to number 80,000 men. Wellington called to his aid the faults of the French supply system. The one thing that a French army could not do was to stay still. Having no machinery to provide food and fodder from long distances, French troops could only live while their foraging parties could find food. If, therefore, they could be brought up against a barrier which they could not force, they would be faced with the alternatives of starvation or retreat. To deal with such an undertaking the Portuguese law was admirably adapted. Every able-bodied man was liable for service either in the Militia, a semi-trained body, useful for garrisoning fortifications, or in the *ordenança* a mass of untrained, poorly armed peasantry. It would be murder to put these ragged levies into the field against trained troops, but in their own districts, knowing every path and patch of cover they could be formidable to stragglers, foraging parties and aides-de-camp. They could also dig and were used in huge numbers to construct the barrier that was to bring the French to a halt. This was the Lines of Torres Vedras across the Lisbon peninsula, on which work had started in October 1809.

This then was the plan. The field army was to retreat before the French army drawing it on into Portugal and administering a salutary check, if the opportunity offered. The country was to be swept clear of inhabitants and provisions in the path of the invader who would eventually come up against the impregnable barrier at Torres Vedras. Then the militia and *ordenança* would close in across his rear and insulate him from Spain and from all sources of food. There was no need to defeat the French in the open field, they would be defeated by starvation.

Throughout the winter of 1809–10 rumour had been strong that Napoleon himself would command the great army that was to drive the English from Portugal. He had enforced peace on his eastern frontiers; his carriages were ordered to Madrid and the Imperial Guard marched to Bayonne. But the Emperor's attention was diverted by his divorce and re-marriage. On 17th April 1810 an Imperial Decree was published naming André Masséna, Marshal of the Empire, Duke of Rivoli and Prince of Essling, as commander of the Army of Portugal.

Masséna was amongst the best of the marshals. Born in 1755 he had served in the ranks of the army of Louis XVI for 14 years, before being honourably discharged and becoming a smuggler across the Franco-Savoyard frontier. He rejoined the army after the Revolution, was elected to the command of a battalion, and three years later was the general commanding the right wing of the Army of Italy when young General Bonaparte arrived to command it in his marvellous campaign of 1796. He was a commander of immense determination, and had rendered signal service to Napoleon by his epic defence of Switzerland against the Austrians and Russians in 1799 and by his long defence of Genoa which made possible the French victory at Marengo. He was immoderately devoted to money and women. His detractors attributed his absence from the battle of Austerlitz to his preoccupation with looting Venice, and it is certain that when he died, two years after Waterloo, he left 40,000,000 francs despite the fact that in 1806, the Emperor had mulcted him of 3,000,000 which he had raised in Livorno by selling licences to trade with England. Few men liked Masséna, and his Italianate looks had not been improved when Napoleon had accidentally blinded him in one eye while shooting.

He joined his new command, accompanied by the sister of one of his aides-de-camp dressed as a hussar, at Salamanca in May, and made no secret of his detestation of his assignment. He was barely mollified by the Emperor's assurance that his reputation alone would suffice to end the war. The new army consisted of three corps whose effective strength totalled little short of 70,000 including more than 8,000 cavalry. A further corps of more than 20,000 men, which had not yet crossed the Pyrenees, was promised for his support and a generous siege-train was making its ponderous way across Spain to join him.

Marshal Ney, the senior corps commander, the bravest and most insubordinate of generals, with his Sixth Corps lay around Salamanca, Reynier, with the Second Corps, was to the south in the valley of the Tagus covering the road to Madrid by Talavera up which the Anglo-Spanish armies had advanced in the previous year, and Junot with the Eighth Corps had (22nd April) just successfully besieged Astorga to the north. Napoleon's orders called for a deliberate advance: 'Tell the Prince of Essling', he had written to Berthier at the end of May, 'that, according to our English intelligence, the army of General Wellington is composed of no more than 24,000 British and Germans, and that his Portuguese are only 25,000 strong. I do not wish to enter Lisbon at this moment, because I could not feed the city, whose immense population is accustomed to live on sea-borne food. He can spend the summer months in taking Ciudad Rodrigo and the Almeida. He need not hurry but can go methodically to work.'

During the first part of the year Wellington was chiefly concerned to rest his troops and to refill the ranks with the convalescents from 'Guadiana fever'. His main force, the First, Third and Fourth Divisions, was held well back from the frontier, billeted in such small comfort as the countryside allowed. Only the Light Division, with the hussars of the German Legion and Ross's troop of Horse Artillery were in contact with the French.

This was a task which Robert Craufurd performed to perfection. He was a bitter, disappointed Scot, five years older than Wellington. Though apt to be impetuous in the face of the enemy, he was one of the rare British officers who had made a serious study of his profession. He was a ruthless disciplinarian, whose savage temper occasionally made him unjust, but he earned the respect and devotion of the other ranks, British and Portuguese, in his division, by his competence in the field and his careful concern for their rations.

From January to June, with five battalions, two of them Portuguese, and his single German regiment of hussars, he held inviolate a front of 50 miles between the Douro and the Sierra de Gata, on the line of the River Agueda. Through his screen no Frenchman ever penetrated; into his hands came the information to build a complete and accurate picture of the order of battle of the whole Army of Portugal. Under his command the Light Division became 'alike the admiration of their friends and foes'. 'Seven minutes sufficed to get it under arms during the nights, a quarter of an hour, day or night, to gather them in order of battle at the alarm posts, with the baggage loaded and assembled at a convenient distance in the rear; and this not upon a concerted signal and as a trial, but all times certain, and for many months consecutively.'

At the beginning of June, Ney's corps laid siege to Ciudad Rodrigo. The garrison of 5,500 Spaniards put up a determined defence. Wellington did not feel able to move to its support. 'With an army one-fourth inferior in numbers, a part of it being of a doubtful description, and at all events but just made, and not more than one-third of the numbers of the enemy's cavalry, it would be an action of some risk to leave our mountains, and bring on a general action in the plains.'

Craufurd was forced to draw back his piquet line from the Agueda to the Azeva rivulet and was reinforced by two regiments of Light Dragoons. The nearest supporting troops were Picton's Third Division at Pinhel and Cole's Fourth Division at Guarda. Behind them again, at Celorico were the First Division and three independent Portuguese brigades. In all Wellington had available only 33,000, a force little more numerous than Ney's corps alone, which now had the 17,000 men of Junot in close touch.

Ciudad Rodrigo surrendered on 10th July, and Craufurd who had been

bickering with the French outposts since the siege began fell back to a
position with his left near the fortress of Almeida and his right on the
Coa. It was a position of extreme danger. The river at his back was
unfordable and crossed by only one long narrow bridge. His division of
3,000 infantry, 800 cavalry and four guns, was menaced by a force which
he calculated at 38,000, and which in fact numbered 47,000. Moreover
he had Wellington's reiterated orders not to 'risk anything beyond the
Coa'.

Early on the morning of 24th July, Ney set out to pin the Light Division
against the river. He brought forward four regiments of cavalry and 32
battalions. Craufurd, as Wellington wrote in a private letter, 'remained
above two hours on his ground after the enemy appeared on his front
before they attacked him, during which time he might have retired across
the Coa twice over'. When Ney finally attacked, Craufurd immediately
lost control of the battle and only the skill of the regimental officers and
the stubborn bravery of the three English battalions saved the division at
a cost of 333 casualties. Ney, then, to prove that French commanders
have their fair share of folly, launched a series of attacks in column across
the narrow bridge under short-range fire from rifles, muskets and artillery.
Before he desisted the French casualties exceeded 500.

Wellington had neither the means nor the wish to fight the Army of
Portugal near the frontier. The disproportion between the two forces was
such as to make the risk of a major engagement unjustifiable. News,
moreover, had reached him that the 18,000 men of the Second Corps
had crossed to the north bank of the Tagus, so that the concentration of
Masséna's army could be quickly achieved. It was therefore necessary to
retreat, imposing as much delay as possible, and rely on geography, winter
and the Portuguese peasantry to compensate for the lack of numbers in
the Allied army.

Masséna, obeying the Emperor's orders to proceed 'methodically',
waited for three weeks before opening trenches against Almeida.
Wellington had hoped that this small fortress, strongly armed and
adequately garrisoned, might delay the French almost as long as Ciudad
Rodrigo had done, 'it will, I hope, make a stout defence: the governor
is an obstinate fellow, and talks of a siege of ninety days'. In this he was
disappointed; on 26th July, the day on which the breaching batteries
opened on the walls, the main magazine exploded, devastating the town,
which surrendered next day. Wellington who had had his army disposed
in the triangle Villa Cortez, Celorico, Guarda, during this second siege,
now began to fall slowly back.

Masséna was still taking his time, and it was more than a fortnight
before, on 15th September, the corps of Ney and Junot advanced from

Almeida. Reynier had, meantime, marched north and was approaching Guarda. The French commander had a choice of three routes before him. The most tempting was the main road from the Spanish frontier to Coimbra on the south bank of the River Mondego, and on this at Ponte de Murcella, where the road crossed the Alva tributary, Wellington had constructed some minor earthworks. To the south of this there was a poor road which ran from Guarda through Castello Branco and reached the Tagus at Villa Velha and was a shorter route to Lisbon than the main road. Masséna chose the third alternative and took a northerly track by Trancoso and Vizeu. Wellington was delighted, 'There are many bad roads in Portugal,' he wrote, 'but the enemy has taken decidedly the worst in the whole kingdom.' Not only had the decision to take the northerly road imposed two days' additional marching on the enemy, but the road led directly to a position where Wellington knew that he could fight with every chance of inflicting a sharp reverse on the French and of blooding his untried Portuguese in conditions of comparative safety.

Masséna, whose decision had been arrived at with the use of a faulty map and with incompetent advice from Portuguese traitors on his staff, was in despair at the delay. His army had set out from Almeida with rations for thirteen days and seven of these were already exhausted before he could move beyond Vizeu. 'It is impossible', he wrote to Paris, 'to find worse roads than these; they bristle with rocks . . . we are marching through a desert; not a soul to be seen anywhere.' A French gunner wrote: 'There is no road, only a stony dangerous mountain track, which the artillery had all the pains in the world to follow without meeting accidents. It is all steep ups and downs. I had to march with a party of gunners ahead of me, with picks and crowbars to enlarge the track.'

Meanwhile Wellington's army was retreating at an almost leisurely pace down the main road. Hill with 10,000 men was moving to join them from the south as was Leith with the 7,000 men of the newly formed Fifth Division. It was not until 24th August that contact between the two armies was regained when men of Reynier's corps drove in the British vedettes near Mortagoa, five miles from Busaco.

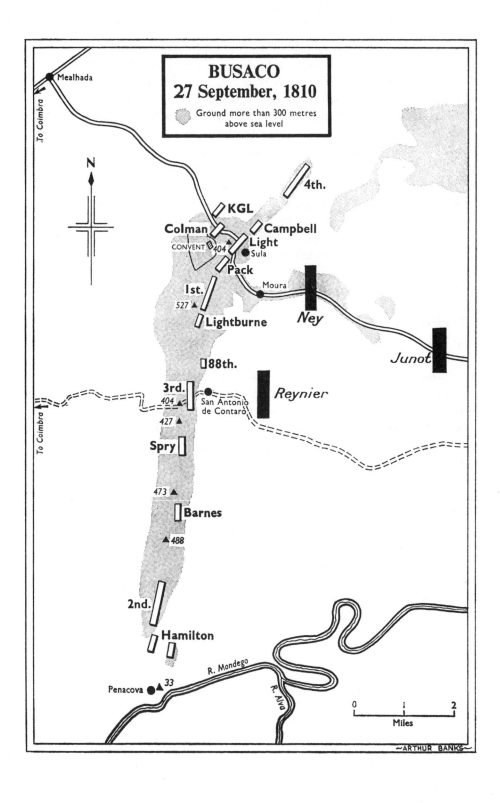

BUSACO
27 September, 1810

Ground more than 300 metres above sea level

Mealhada

To Coimbra

N

4th.

KGL

Colman

Campbell

Light

CONVENT 404

Sula

Pack

1st.

Moura

527

Ney

Lightburne

Junot

88th.

3rd.

404

San Antonio de Contaro

Reynier

427

Spry

To Coimbra

473

Barnes

488

2nd.

Hamilton

R. Mondego

R. Alva

Penacova 33

0   1   2
Miles

~ARTHUR BANKS~

2

Busaco – 27th September 1810

By the night of 25th September, the Anglo-Portuguese army was concentrated on the Serra do Busaco, except for Hill's two divisions (Second British and Hamilton's Portuguese), which were encamped on the south bank of the Mondego, waiting to cross the fords of Penacova at dawn the following morning.

There had been some skirmishing on the 24th and 25th but the British had made no stand. Wellington was not concerned with minor bickerings; his aim was to entice his opponent into attacking him on the magnificent defensive position that lay squarely across the French line of advance.

The Serra do Busaco is a long steep-fronted ridge measuring some ten miles from its southern end which dominates the crossing of the Mondego at Penacova to the point where it shades off into broken country some three miles north of the Carmelite convent of Busaco. A Horse Artillery officer who asked a staff officer for a map of the position to send to England was told, 'You only have to draw a damned long hill, and that will be sufficiently explanatory.' Apart from two tracks towards the southern end, the only roads that cross the Serra are the main Celorico–Coimbra road, which winds up a solitary spur to the north of the convent passing through the villages of Moura and Sula, and a moderate cart-track which climbs the slope above the hamlet of San Antonio de Contaro. Except on the Sula-Moura spur where there are pine woods on the lower reaches, the forward slope is bare of all cover, except for rocky outcrops and a thick covering of heather and gorse. The crest of the ridge undulates having its highest point to the south of the convent, but in general there is a plateau along the crest up to 400 yards wide. Along the reverse slope runs a lateral track which the exertions of British Engineers and Portuguese peasants had made passable for artillery.

Given an army twice the size of that which Wellington commanded the Busaco position would have been impregnable, but with only 50,000 infantry on a 10-mile front, it was impossible to be strong everywhere. At the southern end, above the river, Hill's 10,000 British and Portuguese had a front of two and a half miles, while to their immediate left was a further British brigade, Barnes' from Fifth Division. Thus three British

23

and two Portuguese brigades were available to meet any French move on the right, on whichever side of the river it might come. The left flank was held by Lowry Cole's Fourth Division (4,500 British and 2,800 Portuguese). This was the least secure part of the position since Wellington knew of a country road, bad even by Portuguese standards, that led around the north of the Serra, and which he had no regular troops to guard, while the militia whom he ordered to block it failed to arrive. Within supporting distance of Cole's division was placed the only reserve that could be spared, a brigade of K.G.L. infantry (2,000 strong) and a Portuguese brigade (2,300). The highest point of the ridge was allocated to the three British brigades of the First Division (5,000), while the two roads were blocked by the Light Division (3,800) on the Sulaspur, and the Third Division (4,700) in the Pass of San Antonio. The 4,500 Portuguese from the Fifth Division were posted in the two-mile gap between the powerful forces on the right flank and the Third Division at the pass. During the 25th September Picton had been ordered to detach from the Third Division one British brigade, little more than a thousand strong, to extend the right of the First Division and after dark on the 26th he had himself moved out his strongest British battalion, the 88th, to plug the mile-long gap between his left and the right of his detached brigade. Pack's independent Portuguese brigade (2,700) were formed between the Light and First Divisions in front of the walls of the convent park.

The advance-guard of Reynier's corps leading the French army approached the foot-hills of the Serra on the afternoon of the 25th September, with the Light Division retiring in front of them. At Wellington's insistence no stand was made except in the village of Moura, which was defended by the rear brigade until nightfall, when the Light Division took up its position on the crest of the ridge, leaving only four companies of Rifles in Sula as a *point d'appui* for the skirmishers. Before dark, the vanguard of Ney's corps had reached the neighbourhood of Moura, and Reynier's corps moved south to San Antonio de Contaro.

Next morning, Ney examined the Allied position and formed the impression that while the convent and Coimbra road were held with infantry and artillery, the bulk of Wellington's force was moving north towards Oporto. From this erroneous appreciation, based, it must be supposed, on seeing the Fourth Division taking up its position on the northern end of the Serra, Ney recommended immediate frontal attack and sent an aide-de-camp galloping back ten miles to Masséna's headquarters for endorsement of his plan. Masséna was otherwise engaged but, after a two-hour delay, while the A.D.C. shouted Ney's recommendations to him through his bedroom door, the French commander rode forward, examined the position for himself and issued orders for an attack on the following morning.

Reynier was to advance from San Antonio to attack the Allied right at whichever point on the ridge appeared most accessible, and having reached the crest was to wheel to his right and sweep along the ridge up to the main Coimbra road. Ney was to wait until Reynier was '*maître des hauteurs*' and was then to advance with two of his three divisions up to the line of the Coimbra road. The Eighth Corps was to act as a firm base to the east of Moura with the cavalry in its rear.

There was a fatal flaw to these orders. None of the French commanders had any realistic picture of the strength or position of Wellington's army. They were unaware that three divisions had joined from the south and estimated the Allied infantry strength at no more than 25,000 including Portuguese troops whom they considered a negligible factor. In consequence the point above San Antonio which was chosen for turning the Allied right was scarcely right of the Allied centre and left the divisions of Leith, Hill and Hamilton unoccupied and free to march against Reynier's flank.

That night the Allied army slept in its battle order, and lit no fires. It was bitterly cold as the wind blew in from the Atlantic, and many as they lay down to sleep reflected uneasily that down in the valley was 'the famous French army, the terror of the world, the conqueror of Italy, Spain, Egypt and Germany. It had been victorious at Jena, Austerlitz, Marengo, Ulm, and Vienna, and on the morrow we were going to try conclusions with it.'

At daylight a thick mist hid the French in the valley from their opponents on the heights. The Allies would in any event have been invisible to the French since apart from the light companies which were strung out in skirmishing order on the forward slope, the whole army was concealed behind the crest.

Reynier's corps started up the slope soon after 6 a.m. The 14,600 men were formed into two heavy columns each covered by a thick screen of *tirailleurs*. On the left General Heudelet's division, 15 battalions strong, was aiming to reach the Pass of San Antonio de Contaro, where the road from San Antonio crosses the ridge in a dip between two knolls. On the right General Merle with 12 battalions aimed at a dip about a mile to the north of the pass. Both columns had a front of one company, with the companies of the succeeding battalions line upon line in rear. Almost as soon as they moved forward their *tirailleurs* began pushing back the skirmishers of the light companies of the Third Division, and hearing from the fusillade the width of the front on which he was to be attacked, Picton ordered four companies of the 45th, and a battalion of the 8th Portuguese to reinforce the 88th, on the left of his position. This reinforcement of his left, reduced his force at the pass to one and a half British and two Portuguese battalions, supported by a battery of Portuguese six-pounders, and it was here that the first attack fell. The French 31st regiment, four battalions strong, having outstripped the rest of its column came up the San Antonio road, losing heavily to the artillery. The 74th and the two battalions of the Portuguese 21st regiment drawn up on either side of the guns, opened on it with volleys of musketry and brought it to a halt. The 31st tried repeatedly to deploy, but the musketry was too much for it and the regiment losing its order edged away to its right to avoid the fire of the six-pounders. Nevertheless the French managed to hold their position near the crest.

Meanwhile, about a mile to the north of the pass a more serious threat was developing. Reynier's right-hand column, the 12 battalions of Merle's division, were aiming for the saddle in which the 88th stood alone and unsupported. Low on the forward slope the column had met the light companies of the 45th, 74th and 88th and had driven them back by weight of numbers. It was this firing that had caused Picton to order reinforcements to his northern flank. The light companies fell back south-westerly, and the French, whose sense of direction was confused by the mist, swung off their direct route to follow them. Thus their skirmishers reached a clump of rocks on the crest in a gap between the right of the 88th and the left of the troops at the pass, a gap that was only beginning to be plugged with the arrival from the pass of the half-battalion of 45th and the Portuguese battalion.

All now depended on Colonel Alexander Wallace of the 88th. He sent the commander of his grenadier company, Captain Dunne, 'to the right, where the rocks were highest, to ascertain how matters stood, for he did not wish, at his own peril, to quit the ground he had been ordered to occupy without some strong reason for doing so.

'In a few moments, Dunne returned almost breathless; he said the rocks were filling fast with Frenchmen, that a heavy column was coming up the hill beyond the rocks, and that the four companies of the 45th were about to be attacked. Wallace asked if he thought half the 88th would be able to do the business ? "You will want every man" was the reply.

'Wallace, with a steady but cheerful countenance, turned to his men, and looking them full in the face, said, "Now, Connaught Rangers, mind what you are going to do; pay attention to what I have so often told you, and when I bring you face to face with those French rascals, drive them down the hill – don't give the false touch, but push home to the muzzle! I have nothing more to say, and if I had, it would be of no use, for in a *minit* or two there'll be such an infernal noise about your ears, that you won't be able to hear yourselves."

'Wallace then threw the battalion from line into column, right in front, and moved on our side of the rocky point at a quick pace; on reaching the rocks, he soon found it manifest that Dunne's report was not exaggerated; a number of Frenchmen were in possession of this cluster, and so soon as we approached within range, we were made to appreciate the effects of their fire, for our column was raked from front to rear. The moment was critical but Wallace, without being in the least taken aback, filed out the Grenadier and first battalion companies,* commanded by Captains Dunne and Dansey, and ordered them to storm the rocks, while he took the fifth battalion company, commanded by Captain Oates, also out of the column, and ordered that officer to attack the rocks at the opposite side to that assailed by Dunne and Dansey. This done, Wallace placed himself at the head of the remainder of the 88th, and pressed on to meet the French columns.

'At this moment the four companies of the 45th, commanded by Major Gwynne, a little to the left of the 88th, and in front . . . commenced their fire, but it in no way arrested the advance of the French column, as it with much order and regularity, mounted the hill, which at this point is rather flat. A battalion of the 8th Portuguese infantry, posted on a rising ground, on our right and a little in our rear, in place of advancing with us, opened a distant and ill-directed fire . . . and a battalion of [Portuguese] militia, which was immediately in rear of the 8th Portuguese, took to their heels the moment the first volley was discharged by their own countrymen!

'Wallace threw himself from his horse, and placing himself at the head of the 45th and 88th, ran forward at a charging pace into the midst of the terrible flame in his front. All was now confusion and uproar, smoke, fire and bullets, officers and soldiers, French drummers and French drums knocked down in every direction; British, French and Portuguese mixed together; while in the midst of all was to be seen Wallace, fighting – like his ancestor of old! – at the head of his devoted followers, and calling out to his soldiers to "press forward!" Never was defeat more complete – for Wallace never slackened his fire while a Frenchman was within his reach.

---

* The establishment of a normal infantry battalion (as distinct from Light Infantry and Rifle battalions) was one light company (for skirmishing), one grenadier company (assault troops), and eight 'battalion' companies.

He followed them down the edge of the hill, and then he formed his men in line, waiting for any orders he might receive, or for any fresh body that might attack him.'

Even after the defeat of Merle's column, the front of the Third Division was severely threatened. Foy's brigade had not followed the column which attacked the pass, and while Wallace was chasing his opponents down the forward slope, Foy's seven battalions were establishing themselves on the crest on a small height immediately north of the pass. The first Allied troops sent against him, the remaining companies of the 45th and some Portuguese, made no impression, and the Portuguese became disorganised and demoralised. Reinforcements were quickly on the way. As soon as the mist had cleared, Leith seeing no French to his front, had set the Fifth Division marching to its left, with Hill's division following. Leaving his Portuguese and his artillery to support McKinnon at the pass, he doubled his leading British brigade behind the crest, to support Picton who, still wearing his night-cap, was rallying the Portuguese to protect Mackinnon's left flank.

As Leith with the three battalions of Barnes' brigade approached Foy's position, 'A heavy fire of musketry was being kept up on the heights, the smoke of which prevented a clear view of the state of things. But when the rock forming the high part of the Serra became visible, the enemy appeared to be in full possession of it, and a French officer was in the act of cheering with his hat off, while a continued fire was being kept up from thence, and along the whole face of the slope of the Serra, in a diagonal direction towards its bottom, by the enemy ascending rapidly in successive columns, formed for an attack upon a mass of men belonging to the left battalion of the 8th and the 9th Portuguese, who having been severely pressed, had given way.'

Leith acted immediately. He deployed the 9th in line across the plateau, with the 38th in support in their left rear, and although his third battalion, the Royal Scots, had not come up, charged at the head of the line. The French did not wait for the shock. 'The head of my column', wrote their commander, 'fell back to its right, despite my efforts; I could not get them to deploy, disorder set in, and the 17th and 70th raced downhill in headlong flight.'

This was the end of Reynier's attack; he had only one regiment left in reserve, 23 of his battalions had been chased in disorder from the heights, while the front opposed to him was strongly reinforced from the British right. Hill and the Second Division were forming to support Mackinnon's troops at the pass, and Wellington wearing 'a plain low hat, a white collar, a grey overcoat and a light sword' was on the spot giving his orders. 'If they attempt this point again, Hill, you will give them a volley and charge bayonets; but don't let your people follow them too far down the hill.'

Ney's attack up the line of the main road achieved no more success. Having seen Reynier's men reach the crest, Ney put his corps in motion as Masséna had ordered. His two attacking divisions were separated by the ravine of a dry watercourse. The right division, led by Loison, had easier ground to cover and was first in action. Opposed to him were the five battalions of the Light Division supported by two Horse Artillery batteries.

Craufurd used a very strong skirmishing line of two battalions and it was only with difficulty that Loison could evict them from the village of Sula at the foot of the slope. When by weight of numbers the village was cleared, the French column pushed slowly up the hill using four battalions as skirmishers. Craufurd replied by sending a third battalion forward. As the French came forward the Riflemen and *caçadores* retreated from boulder to boulder, keeping up a constant and damaging fire. 'Whenever the Caçadores got a successful shot, they laughed uproariously as if skirmishing were a source of great amusement to them.' At last when they had almost reached the crest, the bugles sounded and the skirmishers doubled over the crest and reformed in rear.

The French now had no visible enemy before them except the 12 Horse Artillery guns and the solitary figure of Craufurd standing on a rock on the skyline. Unseen to them the 43rd and 52nd were lying down in dead ground behind the crest.

The right-hand company of the 52nd exactly fronted the head of the French column. Its commander, George Napier, left an eye-witness account of the clash. 'General Craufurd himself stood on the brow of the hill watching every movement of the enemy and . . . when . . . the head of the column was within *a very few yards of him* he turned round, came up to the 52nd, and called out, "Now, 52nd, revenge the death of Sir John Moore! Charge, charge! Huzza!" and waving his hat in the air he was answered by a shout that appalled the enemy, and in one instant the brow of the hill bristled with two thousand British bayonets. My company met the head of the French column, and calling to my men to form column of sections to give more force to our rush, we dashed forward. William [Napier] and his friend Captain Lloyd who were upon my right had wheeled up their companies by the left, and thus flanked the French column and poured a well-directed fire into them. Major Arbuthnot who was on my left, did the same with the remaining companies of the 52nd, so that the enemy was beset on both flanks of his column and as you may suppose the slaughter was great. We kept on firing and bayonetting till we reached the bottom, and the enemy passed the brook and fell back on their main body. When we got to the bottom, where a small stream ran between us and the enemy's position, by general consent we all mingled together searching for the wounded. During this cessation of fighting we spoke to each other as though we were the greatest friends. Very soon Lord Wellington, finding we remained, as he thought too long below, ordered the bugles to sound the retreat, and the French general having done the same, off scampered the soldiers of each army and returned to their several positions like a parcel of schoolboys called in from play by their master.'

A single battalion of Loison's division which had inclined to its left avoided the rout of its fellows, only to be similarly treated by a Portuguese battalion from Coleman's brigade.

Ney's second column, Marchand's division, fared no better. Faced with the four line battalions of Pack's Portuguese brigade, screened by their *caçadores* and supported by three field batteries, the French failed to get to close quarters, and was recalled when Loison's attack was repulsed.

Apart from sporadic skirmishing, there was no more fighting. The French had lost about 4,600 men, of whom 900 were killed and 360 made prisoners. One divisional commander, Merle, was wounded, while of the eight brigade commanders who climbed the Serra, one was killed, two wounded and one taken. The Allied casualties evenly divided between British and Portuguese were no more than 1,253, of whom only 200 were killed and 51 missing. The wounded included one brigadier. The bulk of the loss fell upon the Third Division, which lost 473. The Fifth Division suffered nearly 200 casualties, 144 of them in the 8th Portuguese which fought under Picton's command throughout the battle. The Light Division lost no more than 177, while Pack's brigade suffered 138 casualties.

Wellington had achieved his essentially limited aim. He had inflicted a bloody repulse on his opponent and had given confidence to his troops, particularly his untried Portuguese, who had fought nowhere badly and in places admirably. It must be admitted that Masséna had played straight into his hands. There was no reason to attack the Serra, for as the French found on the following day a country road outflanked it to the north. Moreover once committed to the attack, the series of five unco-ordinated assaults by heavy columns up steep slopes gave Wellington every chance to reinforce the points threatened. Masséna had never met British troops before and may have underestimated them, but, since two of his corps commanders had been beaten by them during the previous 10 years, there can be little excuse for his failing to pay them the compliment of discovering where they were stationed before he assaulted them.

Wellington showed his usual skill in choosing a defensive position, though given the French line of advance, the choice cannot have been very difficult. The length of the Serra set him a difficult problem of distributing his strength, and it is possible to feel that he over-insured his centre, by detaching a brigade from the Third Division to strengthen the highest part of the feature already strongly held by the 7,000 British and German troops of the First Division. This resulted in there being only three British battalions, 1,800 men, to fill, with 4,700 Portuguese, the three and a half-mile stretch in which Reynier's attack fell. But, although the early mist gave cover to Reynier's assaults and allowed the French twice to reach the forward crest unseen, the issue was never seriously in doubt, and Wellington, who was remarked as displaying 'as usual, extraordinary circumspection, calm, coolness and presence of mind', always managed to bring up his reinforcements in time to prevent the enemy establishing themselves on top of the Serra.

3

Torres Vedras

The decisive engagement of the war in Portugal was also the shortest and the least bloody. On 14th October a gun mounted in redoubt no. 120 fired a single round to warn Masséna not to press his reconnaissance too close to the Lines of Torres Vedras. The Marshal raised his hat in acknowledgement and retired out of range. He reported to Napoleon: 'The Marshal Prince of Essling has come to the conclusion that he would compromise the army of His Majesty if he were to attack in force lines so formidable.'

Wellington had retired from the Busaco position as soon as he saw that the French were moving round his right flank. The Allied army reinforced by 8,000 Spaniards, were all within the Lines by 10th October. The French advance-guard came up to them the following day, the infantry following on the 12th and 13th. From the start the French regarded the Lines as impregnable. Even Ney 'the bravest of the brave' declined to attack them.

The Lines of Torres Vedras brought the westward flow of the French invasion of Portugal to a permanent halt. Wellington had first ordered their construction in October 1809 and as Masséna throughout the spring and summer of 1810 delayed his advance, the scope of the work of fortification was increased. In their final form the works consisted of three lines. The first two, 29 and 22 miles long respectively, stretched between the Tagus and the sea. The third, a final insurance against unforeseeable disaster, was a two-mile line covering the port of São Julião, at which the army could be embarked. Each line consisted of a series of mutually supporting strongpoints, covered by inundations, abattis and escarpments, existing and contrived, which would make the capture of each one a major and costly operation. Nor was any member of the Anglo-Portuguese field army needed to garrison the strongpoints, for which 20,000 second-line troops were available, and the divisions and independent brigades that had fought at Busaco were held concentrated at strategic points in rear to fall upon any French column that forced its way through the obstacles in its path.

The French position was unenviable. Unable to advance, they were faced with the alternative of staying where they were or of retreating ignominiously. The country around them had been largely swept clear of supplies and in a great arc round the north of their bivouacs, the Portuguese militia and *ordenança* cut off all communication with the outside world. Nevertheless, as General Hill wrote on 10th November 1810 'it is very difficult to starve a Frenchman', and Masséna, with the obstinacy that had characterised his defence of Genoa, held his ground. He had been promised the support of the Ninth Corps and was hoping for co-operation from Soult's army in Andalusia, although he had no means of knowing anything of the movements of either. It was more than a month, until 15th November, before he made a short retreat to a strong position behind the Rio Mayor at Santarem, where he had access to fresh foraging grounds and had some hope of being able to feed his men.

Wellington followed cautiously with part of his army and, as soon as he was convinced that his opponent was establishing himself for a long stay in his new position, settled down to wait until the French moved again. There was nothing to be gained by bringing on a battle. Even if he won it would be a waste of lives. Sooner or later starvation must drive Masséna back. Meanwhile the British army was growing stronger and fitter. While the French combed the countryside for a few potatoes or a bushel of corn, the Royal Navy ensured that regular rations reached the British and Portuguese. Convalescents returned to the regiments from the hospitals, and fresh troops from England enabled the Fifth Division to be given its second British brigade, and the Sixth Division to be formed with the usual two British and one Portuguese brigades.

While the Allied army expanded, Masséna's force steadily shrank. Of the 65,000 men who had been present at Busaco, fewer than 47,000 were with the eagles in the New Year. This more than compensated for 8,000 men of the Ninth Corps who joined Masséna under d'Erlon at the end of November, and who, though they brought a welcome convoy of ammunition, only aggravated the problem of feeding the army.

Eventually, early in March, even Masséna had to admit defeat and retire. He did so not knowing that at last the Army of the South had moved to his support. At the end of January Soult with nearly 20,000 men had besieged Badajoz, commanding the southern high-road into Portugal. In mid-February he defeated a Spanish army of relief on the Gebora, and on 9th March, four days after Masséna had started his retreat, Badajoz was betrayed to the French. Soult did not enjoy his success for long. Hardly had he entered the town when news reached him that part of the garrison of Cadiz had made a sea-borne sally, and that at Barrosa, Graham with 5,000 British troops had heavily defeated Marshal Victor with 7,000 while 10,000 Spaniards stood idly watching.

Masséna's plan had been to fall back over the Mondego and establish himself on the unravaged ground between Coimbra and Oporto, but so resolute was the appearance of a handful of Portuguese militia at the crossings of the Mondego, that the French army swung east and made for Spain. Their rear was covered by Ney's corps and for a fortnight there was a series of brisk rear-guard actions.

Wellington was unfortunate in that Robert Craufurd, the natural commander of his vanguard, was on leave in England, and command of the Light Division and the advance cavalry, fell to Sir William Erskine, an officer foisted on Wellington by the Horse Guards, on whose posting to Portugal the Adjutant-General wrote: 'No doubt he is sometimes a little mad, but in his lucid intervals he is an uncommonly clever fellow; and I trust he will have no fit during the campaign though he looked a little wild as he embarked.' The pursuit of Masséna was not one of Sir William's lucid intervals; at Casal Novo he flung the 52nd through a thick mist, against the 11 battalions of Marchand's division; at Foz do Arouce he missed an excellent chance of destroying three of Ney's brigades which he found unprepared with an impassable river crossed by only a single narrow bridge at their backs. 'There is', wrote Wellington of him later, 'nothing so stupid as "a gallant officer".' Fortunately the British regiments of the Light Division, trained by Moore and Craufurd, were more than equal to their fumbling temporary commander and harried Ney's corps unmercifully.

On 15th March Masséna decided to cut his losses and run for the Spanish frontier. All the baggage and transport animals were destroyed and the French rear-guard drew increasingly far away from the British advance, which was weakened and retarded by an almost complete failure of supplies while their base was shifted from Lisbon to Figueira, at the mouth of the Mondego. The Portuguese troops whose commissariat was notoriously sketchy, suffered the most. The British commander of a Portuguese brigade wrote pathetically to the Quartermaster-General, 'The bearer, our Commissary, says that there is nothing to be got in Coimbra, and I wish to God you could tell him or me what to do. The men have had neither bread nor meat yesterday or today, and very little indeed the day before. I really dread our coming to a complete stand still. Indeed, honestly to speak, I do not see how the men can march.'

Masséna made a last, desperate attempt to save himself from being hunted out of Portugal. From Guarda he decided to advance south-west towards central Portugal. It was an absurd scheme as the army had no wagons, no mules and no food. Ney refused to attempt it and was sent back to France in disgrace. Within a week the whole army knew he had been right and the Army of Portugal moved back to the east bank of the Coa, in touch with supplies from Ciudad Rodrigo and the fertile plains of Leon.

Even then they still offered Wellington a chance for offensive action. The Second Corps on the French left was unsupported on a ridge behind the Coa at Sabugal. Wellington gave orders to turn it with the Light Division and cavalry while four other divisions struck at it in front. Despite Sir William Erskine, who launched the Light Division in the wrong direction in thick mist, while he himself vanished with the cavalry in another wrong direction, the French on 7th April were driven off with 750 casualties against a British loss of 170. Wellington described the action as 'one of the most glorious that British troops were ever engaged in'.

After Sabugal, the only French troops left in Portugal were the garrison of Almeida. Masséna's Portuguese expedition had cost him 25,000 men, 9,000 horses and all but 36 of his wagons. But this was not enough to break down that commander's obstinacy. Retiring behind Ciudad Rodrigo he rapidly reorganised his army, borrowed some cavalry and gun-teams from the Army of the North, and less than a month after Sabugal, struck again at the Allies in an attempt to relieve Almeida.

His first attempt on 3rd May was a complete failure. Having, apparently, learned nothing at Busaco, he tried to storm the village of Fuentes de Oñoro by frontal attack in column and was checked with heavy loss. Two days later, he brought his undoubted military skill to bear on the situation, and turned Wellington's right with a strong force of cavalry supported by three divisions of infantry, while once more heavy columns vainly assaulted the village. In the broad marshy valley on the Allied right there were only 1,400 cavalrymen, Bull's troop of Horse Artillery and the newly formed Seventh Division, seven battalions, only one of which was British.

The French dragoons crashed through a party of Spanish *guerrilleros* on the extreme southern flank and bore down on the Allied infantry. A volley from the Chasseurs Britanniques, a regiment of French *émigrés* in British pay, held them back momentarily, but the massed French infantry was close behind and the Seventh Division was forced to embark on a long, dangerous retreat.

As soon as Wellington realised the danger to his flank, he set Craufurd and Light Division marching to cover the retreat of the Seventh. Without opposition they occupied a wood between the French infantry and their prey. Under cover of this diversion the Seventh had time to reach the safety of the west bank of the Turmes stream. Now it was time for the Light Division to fall back on the main position. Under cover of some companies of Rifles and *caçadores*, they formed up by battalions, with Bull's guns in the intervals. Then, in 'column at quarter distance ready to form square at any moment if charged by cavalry', they set off to cover the three miles that lay between them and safety. Three thousand French horsemen hovered round them, but both sides knew that no cavalry could break steady infantry in square. The small force of British and German cavalry charged again and again. 'Our men', wrote a cornet of the 14th Light Dragoons, 'had *evidently* the advantage as individuals. Their broadswords, ably wielded, flashed over the Frenchmen's heads, and obliged them to cower over their saddlebows. The alarm was indeed greater than the hurt, for their cloaks were so well rolled across their left shoulders, that it was no easy matter to give a mortal stroke with the broad edge of a sabre, whereas their swords were straight and pointed, though their effect on the eyes was less formidable, were capable of inflicting a much severer wound. Many, however, turned their horses, and our men shouted in the pursuit; but it was quite clear that, go which way they might, we were but scattered drops amid their host, and could not possibly arrest their progress.'

If the French came too close, Bull's guns would unlimber and fire a few rounds at close range. At one time two guns were cut off and surrounded. The tired British dragoons made another partial charge, and the French being checked, 'A great commotion was observed in their main body; men and horses were seen to close with confusion and tumult towards one point, where a thick dust and loud cries, and the sparkling of blades, and the flashing of pistols, indicated some extraordinary occurence. Suddenly the multitude became violently agitated, an English shout pealed high and clear, and Norman Ramsey burst forth sword in hand at the head of his battery,★ his horses breathing fire, stretched like greyhounds along the plain, the guns bounded behind like things of no weight, and the mounted gunners followed close, with heads bent low and pointed weapons, in desperate career.'

By the time that the division had reached the ridge west of the village of Fuentes, Wellington had swung his line of battle through a right angle and presented a front to the French which Masséna declined to attack. It had been a critical moment, and Wellington admitted that 'If Boney had been there, we would have been damnably licked'. But Boney was not there, and Wellington knew that he had only the tired Masséna to compete with, supported by troops disheartened by their ill-success in Portugal and having lost faith in their commander.

A week later, Marshal Marmont arrived to supersede Masséna. Although he was an unattractive character, it is hard not to feel sorry for Masséna. Given the quality of his opponent, the hostility of the

---

★ It was, in fact, not a battery but a 'division' of two guns.

Portuguese people, the sweeping bare of the countryside, and the unexpected impregnability of the Lines of Torres Vedras, it is clear that his task was impossible from the outset. He made a series of serious blunders, his frontal attacks at Busaco and on the village of Fuentes, his abortive expedition south-west from Guarda, and his negligence in leaving at Coimbra 4,000 wounded inadequately protected against the Portuguese militia, but his obstinacy got nearer to success than could have been hoped for from any other of Napoleon's marshals. Wellington believed that the French could not conquer Portugal with fewer than 100,000 men, Masséna started with 65,000 men and rather more than 10,000 joined him during the campaign. But even if he had been given the larger number it is more than doubtful if he could have succeeded. At 65,000 the Army of Portugal was large enough to defeat the Allied field army if it caught it in open country, but this was exactly the situation which Wellington was determined to prevent. It was by starvation rather than musketry that Wellington had resolved to beat Masséna, and 35,000 additional Frenchmen, trying to live on the gleanings of the artificially barren countryside of northern Estremadura would have aggravated rather than eased Masséna's problem.

Wellington had every reason for satisfaction with the campaign. Everything had gone as he planned. He had inflicted two major defeats on the French, beside a host of smaller ones. Portugal was cleared of the enemy who never again attempted a serious invasion. His British regiments were full of confidence and had suffered only light losses and his Portuguese were shaping into reliable troops.

PART TWO

Wellington and Marmont

4

The Fortresses

As soon as he knew that Masséna was retiring behind Ciudad Rodrigo, Wellington rode south to deal with a new danger. Hill's corps, commanded while he was sick by Beresford and strengthened by the Fourth Division, had marched south during March and April to besiege Badajoz. The town had been invested on 7th May. Soult's reaction had been swift. Gathering a field army of 25,000 men, he had crossed the Sierra Morena and marched to the relief of the threatened garrison. Reinforced by 14,000 Spaniards, Beresford drew up his army to meet him on the ridge of Albuera. In the battle fought there on 16th May Beresford's personal bravery was only rivalled by his inability to handle his troops. Nevertheless, the initiative of his subordinates and the stubborn bravery of his five brigades of British and German infantry were sufficient to drive Soult back over the Sierra. The cost was appalling. Of 7,640 British infantry present, 3,933 were casualties. Wellington arriving on the scene three days later found Beresford overcome with 'the slaughter about him and the vast responsibility'. His report 'was quite in a desponding tone . . . and I said directly, this won't do, write me down a victory. The despatch was altered accordingly.'

Although Hill returned to his command at the end of May, Wellington stayed in the south to supervise the reinvestment of Badajoz. He immediately called down two further divisions from the north. He rightly felt that the Army of Portugal, after its experiences in the retreat from Santarem and the battles of Sabugal and Fuentes de Oñoro, would not be a danger for a few weeks.

That army had, in the meanwhile, received a new commander, Auguste Frédéric Louis Viesse de Marmont, Marshal Duke of Ragusa. Marmont was a complete contrast to Masséna, who was recalled to France in ill-merited disgrace. Coming from a rich *bourgeois* family, his father being an iron-master, he had been an artillery cadet before the Revolution. As a lieutenant he had served with Bonaparte at the siege of Toulon and had been his aide-de-camp in the great Italian campaign. From then on his rise had been rapid. He had commanded the artillery at Marengo, a corps at Wagram and had been responsible for the organisation and a much-needed rationalisation of the artillery of the Imperial armies. Since

1805 he had spent much of his time as Governor of Dalmatia, where he had made himself beloved among the peasantry by supervising major projects for road-building and irrigation. His coming was much welcomed in Spain for unlike Masséna he kept a good table and was careful of the well-being of his troops. Although in 1811 he was only 37, five years younger than Wellington, he had a great reputation as an organiser and had one creditable campaign against the Austrians to his credit as an independent commander.

Marmont's other virtue was a rare one amongst the Marshals. He was sincerely anxious to assist his brother commanders. Hardly had he assumed his command than he detached d'Erlon with 10,000 men to assist Soult, and early in June he marched south with his entire force. He had spent the intervening weeks in reorganising his army, disbanding the cumbersome and inconvenient corps structure and forming the troops into six divisions. He also dispensed with the services of all but two of the former divisional commanders. The frontier of Leon he handed over to Marshal Bessières, commander of the Army of the North, who accepted the charge with the worst possible grace.

Meanwhile Wellington had been attempting to take Badajoz with ludicrously inadequate means, a siege-train of seventeenth-century Portuguese cannon and 45 engineers of all ranks. Two assaults had failed when the combined armies of Marmont and Soult concentrated against him, 60,000 strong. Although the entire Anglo-Portuguese army had moved to the south, leaving the Agueda frontier to the care of the Portuguese Militia, the siege had to be raised. The Allies took up a strong position between the Gebora river and the fortress of Elvas. The two marshals declined to attack and after a few weeks marched away, Soult to put down a Spanish outbreak in Andalusia, Marmont to find food in the country west of Madrid.

Wellington took the main army north again and imposed a distant and partial blockade on Ciudad Rodrigo. A siege-train had, at last, reached Lisbon from England in June and arrangements were being made for its laborious journey to Almeida, which it could not reach before Christmas. The blockaded town was provisioned until October and the front was quiet until late September when Marmont advanced with a force drawn from the Armies of Portugal and the North, numbering 58,000, to throw in further supplies. Wellington, not being prepared to risk a general action, withdrew his forward troops a short distance but, with less than his usual caution, did not concentrate his army.

Marmont did not intend to fight on the west bank of the Agueda, but he sent out a strong cavalry reconnaissance which, to his surprise, found the Allies were widely dispersed. Unwilling to miss a chance, he ordered an advance. The Third Division was found spread over a front of six miles and would have been destroyed in detail but for a magnificent covering action at El Bodon by the 5th Fusiliers and the 77th Regiment. This check made Marmont more than ever cautious and Wellington was able, by a narrow margin, to concentrate six divisions in an impregnable position in front of Alfayates, seeing which the French withdrew. 'It was very pretty,' wrote Graham, newly arrived as second in command of the army, 'but rather fine spun; if the French had behaved with common spirit we should not have got away so easily.'

With Rodrigo supplied, the French armies dispersed in search of food. The Army of the North moved north of the Douro, leaving one division in advance at Salamanca. The Army of Portugal retired to the valley of the Tagus. This put them in a central position, able to move north or south should Wellington threaten either Badajoz or Ciudad Rodrigo. Communications with Soult were tenuous being dependent on a division of the Army of the South stationed at Merida, which was badly mauled when Rowland Hill caught one of its brigades unawares during a brilliant raid to Arroyo dos Molinos at the end of October.

Wellington renewed his distant blockade of Rodrigo with three divisions, while the rest of the army went into winter quarters around Guarda, under the command of General Graham, the victor of Barrosa, who although 63, 21 years older than Wellington, was a most welcome addition to the army.

While Wellington watched for an opportunity to besiege Rodrigo, the siege-train was being moved, with infinite labour, to the fortress of Almeida, which it reached by Christmas. Simultaneously orders from Paris gave the British commander his chance. Napoleon became obsessed with the importance of subduing Valencia, and ordered Marmont to detach 10,000 men to assist Marshal Suchet with this irrelevant task. This force, more than a quarter of his effective strength, marched eastward at the beginning of December. Three weeks later the Emperor withdrew two divisions from the Army of the North now under Dorsenne, and ordered the Army of Portugal to assume responsibility for the whole north-eastern quarter of Spain, north of the Tagus. There was, said Napoleon, no danger from Wellington, whom he believed to have only 20,000 British effectives. To help him to carry out his new responsibilities Marmont was given two divisions from Dorsenne's army, one of which could not, by Imperial order, be withdrawn from the Asturias.

Leaving one division in the Tagus valley, Marmont ordered his three remaining divisions to march northward and rode ahead to meet Dorsenne at Valladolid. Hardly had he arrived, when news reached him that Wellington had invested Ciudad Rodrigo six days earlier.

As soon as Wellington was certain that the Army of Portugal was making a large detachment to help Suchet, he decided to strike. By 5th January the main army was concentrated along the Agueda. There snow and sleet, turning the roads to impassable mud, held up the movement of the siege-train for two days, but on the 8th the town was closely invested and that night John Colborne with 450 volunteers from the Light Division seized an outwork on a commanding height 600 yards from the walls.

Although Rodrigo was not a first-class fortress, it was a sufficiently formidable work. The defences consisted basically of a mediaeval wall, 32 feet high, but this had been improved with an indented *faussebraie* and a ditch with a 12-foot counterscarp of masonry. The garrison, two battalions with about 1,700 men, was rather too small, but the town's armament was enormous. By some oversight, the entire siege-train of the Army of Portugal was stored within the walls and 153 heavy guns with a lavish supply of ammunition were available, although there were only 15 more gunners than guns.

Four divisions took their turns in the trenches, while the remaining three formed the covering force. Reliefs took place at first light, the troops fording the Agueda on their way to and from their work. This, in itself, was not the least of the dangers of their work. 'Pieces of ice that were constantly carried down this rapid stream bruised our men so much, that to obviate it the cavalry . . . were ordered to form four deep across the ford, under the lee of whom we crossed comparatively unharmed, although by the time we reached our quarters our clothes were frozen into a mass of ice.'

Nevertheless the work proceeded briskly and on the afternoon of 14th January, the day on which Marmont first heard of the siege, a battery of 24 heavy guns opened on the weak portion of the wall where Ney had opened a breach in 1810. Four days later, a smaller battery opened fire on another section, 300 yards to the left of the main breach. Next day, Wellington's orders began 'the attack on Ciudad Rodrigo must be made this evening at 7 o'clock'. The main breach was to be assaulted by the Third Division, while the Light attacked the smaller.

Some days earlier Captain George Napier of the 52nd had gone to General Craufurd and 'asked him as a favour that he would allow me to command the storming party . . . . This he promised, and on January 19 . . . I went to [the] three regiments . . . and said, "soldiers, I have the honour to be appointed to the command of the storming party for the assault of the small breach. I want one hundred volunteers from each regiment; those who will go with me come forward." Instantly there rushed out half the division, and we were obliged to take them at chance. I formed them into companies of one hundred men each . . . These were preceded by what is called the *forlorn hope* consisting of twenty-five men, two sergeants and one subaltern, a lieutenant, because if he survives he gets a company. When it was nearly dark the Light Division was formed behind the old convent . . . nearly opposite the small breach. Lord Wellington sent for Colonel Colborne and myself, and pointing out, as well as the light would permit, the spot where the foot of the breach was, he said to me, "Now do you understand the way you are to lead, so as to arrive at the breach without noise or confusion?" I answered, and we went back to the regiment, and just before I moved on some staff officer present said, "Why, your men are not loaded; why do you not make them load?" I replied, "Because if we do not do the business with the bayonet we shall not be able to do it at all, so I shall not load." I heard Lord Wellington, who was close by, say, "Let him alone; let him go his own way".' Promptly at seven o'clock the storming-party advanced 'in double column of sections, Lieutenant Gurwood in advance a few yards with the forlorn hope. We soon came to the ditch, and immediately jumping in, we rushed forward to the *faussebraie*, and having clamboured up we proceded towards the breach. But Lieutenant Gurwood and party, having owing to the darkness of the night, gone too far to the left, was employed in placing ladders on the unbreached face of the bastion, when he got a shot in the head; but immediately recovering his feet he came up to me, and at that moment the engineer . . . called out, "You are wrong, this way to the right is the breach"; and Captain Fergusson, myself, Gurwood, and the rest of the officers, and such men as were nearest . . . rushed on, and we all mounted the breach together, the enemy pouring a heavy fire on us. When about two-thirds up, I received a grape-shot which smashed my elbow and great part of my arm, the men, who thought I was killed, checked for a few moments and . . . commenced snapping their muskets. I immediately called out, "Recollect you are not loaded; push on with the bayonet." Upon this the whole gave a loud "hurrah", and driving all before them carried the breach.'

Almost at the same moment, the Third Division fought their way through the main breach. The governor surrendered the town at once, and there followed a night of plunder and drunkenness.

Marmont, who hoped to have a relieving army concentrated at Salamanca by 1st February, heard the news of the fall on 21st January when he was still between Salamanca and Valladolid, with only 15,000 men available.

Wellington had captured one of the two gateways from Portugal into Spain, for the loss of 1,100 men, of whom fewer than 200 were killed.

The most serious part of his loss was the mortal wounding of Robert Craufurd, the irreplaceable commander of the outposts.

On the morning after the storm of Rodrigo, General Picton passed the bivouac of the Connaught Rangers. 'Some of the soldiers, who were more than usually elevated in spirits, on his passing them, called out, "Well, general, we gave *you* a cheer last night; it is *your* turn *now*." The general, smiling took off his hat and said, "Here, then, you drunken set of brave rascals, *Hurrah, we'll soon be at Badajoz!*" Five days later the siege-guns began their journey to the Guadiana.

Marmont realised that Badajoz would be Wellington's next target. That fortress was the responsibility of the Army of the South, but Marmont knew that Soult could not collect a field force large enough to resist the main Allied army unless he abandoned Andalusia and Murcia to the Spaniards. He therefore proposed to move the bulk of the Army of Portugal, including the two divisions which were due to return from the Valencian expedition, to help Soult. This was forbidden by the Emperor. Only one division could be left by the Tagus. Another was to be transferred to the Army of the North, and the remainder must be held in Leon for a thrust into Beira. 'Your posture should be offensive, with Salamanca as base and Almeida as objective . . . I suppose you consider the English mad, for you believe them capable of marching against Badajoz when you are at Salamanca.'

Before these orders had reached Marmont, the Allied army had started to march south. By mid-March every infantryman of the Anglo-Portuguese army was concentrated around Elvas. The line of the Agueda was held by a single regiment of German Hussars, backed by Portuguese Militia and some Spanish levies.

Badajoz was a far more formidable work than Ciudad Rodrigo. Its northern front is protected by the river Guadiana, 300 yards wide, the eastern side is given some cover by the Rivillas stream which had been dammed to inundate the low ground at the south-eastern angle of the walls, and the junction of the Guadiana and the Rivillas was dominated by the castle, standing on a sharp hill within the town walls which were nowhere less than 23 feet high, with frequent 30-foot bastions. There were three major detached works, the Pardaleras fort, standing on a hill which dominated the southern wall, the San Cristobal on the far bank of the Guadiana, and the Picurina, a powerful redoubt which was separated from the town by inundation and in contact with the garrison only by the dam across the Rivillas which was protected by a small work, known as the San Roque *lunette*.

The governor, General Philippon, was well known to both armies for his gallantry and determination and he had an adequate garrison of seven French infantry battalions totalling 4,700 men.

Wellington decided to attack the south-eastern corner of the walls. This necessitated the capture of the Picurina fort which after six days' battering was stormed on the night of 25th March. Work could then be started on the main business of building batteries to breach the town walls, and by 5th April, three breaches were reckoned practicable. The assault had to be postponed until the following night, when the Fourth and Light Divisions were detailed for the assault on the breaches. Several diversionary attacks were planned at distant parts of the wall and at the request of their commanders, the Third and Fifth Divisions were ordered to attempt to break in by escalade, the Third at the castle, the Fifth near the river at the north-west corner of the town.

At the breaches, the storming parties crept forward silently and apparently unobserved. 'All was hushed and the town lay buried in gloom; the ladders were placed in the edge of the ditch, when suddenly an explosion took place at the foot of the breaches, and a burst of light disclosed the whole scene – the earth seemed to rock under us – what a sight. The ramparts crowded with the enemy – the French soldiers standing on the parapets – the fourth division advancing rapidly in column of companies on a half circle to our right, while a short-lived glare from the barrels of powder and combustibles flying into the air gave to friends and foes a look as if both bodies of troops were laughing at each other.

'A tremendous firing now opened upon us, and for an instant we were stationary; but the troops were *no ways daunted*. The ladders were found exactly opposite the centre breach and the whole division rushed to the assault with the most amazing resolution. There was no check. The soldiers flew down the ladders, and the cheering from both sides was loud and full of confidence . . . . Grapeshot and musketry tore open their ranks. The ditch was very wide, and when arrived at the foot of the centre breach, eighty or ninety men were formed. It was a volcano! . . . Up we went; some killed, and others impaled on the bayonets of their own comrades or hurled headlong, French soldiers standing upon the walls, taunting and inviting our men to come up and try it again.'

'The breach was covered by a breastwork from behind, and was ably defended on the top by *chevaux-de-frises* of sword-blades sharp as razors, chained to the ground; while the ascent to the top of the breach was covered with planks with sharp nails in them.' Time and again the Fourth and Light Divisions struggled to the top of the breach, but it was impossible to surmount the obstacles or to withstand the fire. They fell back to their starting-point. 'At this moment,' wrote the senior medical officer of the army, 'I cast my eyes on Lord Wellington lit by the glare of a torch held by Lord March . . . the jaw had fallen, and the face was of unusual length, while the torchlight gave his countenance a lurid aspect; but still the expression of his face was firm.'

Against all probability the operation was saved by the two escalading divisions. The Third, although Picton was wounded at an early stage, filed over the narrow milldam across the Rivillas under 'streams of fire' and dashing to the top of the castle mound raised five ladders against the castle walls. 'The whole face of the wall,' wrote the assistant engineer, who was guiding them, 'being opposed by the guns of the citadel, was so swept by their discharges of round-shot, broken shells, bundles of cartridges, and other missiles, and also from the top of the wall, ignited shells, &c., that it was almost impossible to twinkle an eye on any man before he was knocked down. In such an extremity, four of my ladders with troops on them, and an officer on the top of each were broken, successively, near the upper ends, and slided into the angle of the abutment. On the remaining ladder was no officer; but, a private soldier at the top, in attempting to go over the wall, was shot in the head, as soon as he appeared over the parapet, and tumbled backwards to the ground; when the next man (45th regiment) to him upon the ladder instantly sprang over! ! ! ! I instantly cheered, "Huzza, there is one man up".' The 45th gained a foothold on the battlements and held it long enough for the fallen ladders to be raised again. The Third Division poured into the castle and subdued the defenders who fought a gallant and desperate battle, defending the keep stair by stair until they were annihilated.

But although the castle was in British hands, its assailants would have had to make a second assault to fight their way through its defences into the town, and already the bugles of the Fifth Division were sounding in the streets. General Leith and his men had started to their assault an hour late, and it was past eleven o'clock before the assault was able to begin. Their objective was the bastion of San Vicente, which 'had an escarpe thirty-one feet six inches in height, flanked by artillery, the pallisades of the covered way were entire, – the counterscarp nearly twelve feet deep, and in the ditch, a cunette, five feet six inches in depth, and six feet six inches in breadth had been excavated'.

The French opened fire as the Fifth mounted the glacis, but the defenders had been thinned to meet the threat at the breaches and the assailants were able to press up to the foot of the wall. 'At first, few of the ladders could be placed, some of them after being reared, were thrown from the walls back into the ditch. Others constructed of green wood opened and separated, or were not of sufficient length, consequently the troops forced in by means of only three or four.' But force in they did, and pushing through the street, opened fire against the backs of the defenders of the breach.

As soon as Wellington heard this news he ordered a new assault on the breaches. 'We moved back to the bloody work as if nothing had happened. We entered the ditches, and passed over the bodies of our brave fellows who had fallen and dashed forward to the breaches. Only a few random shots were now fired, and we entered without opposition.'

The troops, maddened by their losses, subjected Badajoz to three dreadful days of sack. It had never been a popular town with the British, being thought to have pro-French sympathies, but nothing could have excused the orgy of plunder, rape and arson that overwhelmed the town.

The siege had cost the Allies almost 5,000 casualties, of whom 3,700 fell in the storm. The Fourth and Light Divisions each lost more than 900 men from the British regiments alone, and the Third and Fifth each more than 500. Visiting the scene next morning, a surgeon saw that at the main breach, 'there lay a frightful heap of thirteen or fifteen hundred British soldiers, many dead but still warm, mixed with the desperately wounded, to whom no assistance could yet be given. There lay the burned and blackened corpses of those who had perished by the explosions, mixed with those that were torn to pieces by round shot or grape, and killed by musketry, stiffening in the gore, body piled upon body, involved and intertwined into one hideous mass of carnage. The smell of burning flesh was yet shockingly strong and disgusting.'

'The capture of Badajoz', wrote Wellington to the Secretary of State, 'affords as strong an instance of the gallantry of our troops as has ever been displayed. But I greatly hope that I shall never again be the instrument of putting them to such a test as they were put to last night.'

The French armies had been able to do nothing to help the garrison. Soult, having cut the Andalusian garrisons to the bone, reached Villa Franca on the day after Badajoz had fallen. He had managed to gather a force of 25,000 and found himself faced with Wellington's covering force of 31,000 men strongly posted on the Albuera position. He immediately counter-marched to deal with the Spanish armies which had emerged from the sierras as soon as he had gone north. Marmont and the Army of Portugal loyally, but without hope, carried out the Emperor's orders to invade Beira. There was no chance of success. A few Portuguese villages were burned to the ground, some militia were given a sharp lesson at Guarda, before Marmont with his men on the edge of starvation, retreated slowly into Spain. On his retreat he narrowly avoided being cut off by Wellington returning to the Agueda with the main body of the army.

5

The Plains of Leon

Wellington had seized the initiative with Ciudad Rodrigo and Badajoz. Holding the two gateways between Spain and Portugal he could choose his point of attack. He had also received substantial cavalry reinforcements, three British and two German regiments, which enabled him to operate with more confidence in open country. Two armies lay directly opposed to him: Soult, south of the Tagus, and Marmont to the north of that river. The Army of the South was isolated and vulnerable but Wellington decided that it would be more profitable to attack the Army of Portugal, since if that could be driven back Soult must retire or be cut off from all the other armies. Rowland Hill with his usual corps was therefore left to watch the southern frontiers of Portugal.

The French armies in Spain had, for the first time since the invasion of the Peninsula, considerably decreased in size. In May 1812 they totalled only 230,000. Part of this decline was due to the normal wastage of men in a bitterly hostile country, but the largest single cause was the forthcoming invasion of Russia. For this Napoleon had withdrawn 27,000 men of the Guard and the Polish regiments. His forthcoming departure for the east had also induced the Emperor for the first time to place the command in Spain in the hands of his brother Joseph, with the veteran Marshal Jourdan as Chief of Staff. This centralisation was long overdue, but was not at first effective. The commanders of the outlying armies had been independent too long to relish control from Madrid, and Joseph's first set of instructions, a sensible plan to establish a central reserve, was rejected, with varying degrees of civility, by all those to whom it was addressed. Nevertheless, Wellington could not afford to neglect the other French armies while he dealt with the Army of Portugal. If they were sufficiently endangered they must eventually give up their occupation duties and combine against him in overwhelming strength. Each therefore had some diversion arranged for its benefit. The Army of the South, 54,000 strong, was already fully occupied by the siege of Cadiz. Lest its available field force should attempt to help Marmont, Spanish armies, under Ballasteros, were to demonstrate in the plains, while carefully avoiding battle, a task performed with singular ineptitude. Fortunately Soult's natural disinclination to help his colleagues achieved the desired purpose. A sea-borne expedition from Sicily, consisting of British and Neapolitan troops, was to keep Suchet and the 60,000 men of the Army of Aragon in play. Here again, the plan miscarried and the landing did not take place until the end of July, but since French intelligence agents had reported the assembly of the transports in Sicily early in June, Suchet felt justified in refusing to assist the main operation throughout the vital period. The Army of the North had 48,000 men, and although its primary task was to keep the communications with France clear of the guerrillas which beset them, it was required by the Emperor to reinforce Marmont with two divisions should he be attacked. For the benefit of this army and its new commander, Caffarelli, Wellington arranged the most successful of his diversions. Commodore Sir Home Popham, with two ships of the line, seven smaller ships of war and two battalions of Royal Marines was to cruise along the northern coast of Spain, keeping in touch with the guerrillas and occasionally landing to seize a fortress using guns landed from the ships as a battering-train. As soon as the French sent a strong column to relieve or retake the selected fortresses, the Spaniards would return to their mountain fortresses and the fleet would move down the coast, call down another guerrilla and besiege another fortress. This scheme worked to perfection and the Army of the North spent the summer months marching up and down the coast trying hopelessly to march faster than a ship could sail.

There remained only the Army of the Centre, a force of only 18,000 men, whose task was to keep King Joseph's capital and the surrounding provinces safe. This was the most difficult of the armies to distract, being in country unsuitable for large-scale guerrilla activity and out of reach of sea-borne threats. Against them Wellington could no do more than request the Spanish to create as much trouble as was possible without incurring serious reprisals.

Having thus ensured that Marmont was left to his own devices, Wellington concentrated his army on the Agueda in early June. The force consisted of 45,000 Anglo-Portuguese troops, 3,500 of this number cavalry, all of it British and German, and there was a rather thin provision of 54 guns. Co-operating with the army was a small Spanish division, under a French *émigré* officer, Don Carlos de España. On the north bank of the Douro, a flanking force of four Portuguese militia regiments with a brigade of Portuguese dragoons was ready to advance and blockade the outlying French fortress at Astorga.

The field force of the Army of Portugal consisted of 48,000 men in eight divisions, but they were spread out, on orders from Paris, between Oviedo and Avila. One division only was forward at Salamanca, and the division which Napoleon had insisted on posting in the Asturias could hardly come up with the rest of the army in less than three weeks.

The Allies crossed the Agueda on 13th June and met with no opposition until they drove in French videttes a few miles from Salamanca two days later. The French division retired at once leaving behind a garrison of 800 men in three fortified convents which dominated the town bridge over the Tormes. Leaving the Sixth Division to besiege the convents Wellington drew up the remainder of the army on a line of hills between San Cristobal and Cabrerizos, a few miles north of the city.

By 19th June Marmont had concentrated 40,000 men with 80 guns at Fuente Sauco, 20 miles north-east of Salamanca. He also sent urgently to the Army of the North for the two divisions which had been promised to him, and called on Madrid for help. Finding that Wellington was waiting in front of Salamanca he cautiously advanced and made a show of strength in front of the San Cristobal position.

For a time on 20th June it seemed that he was going to oblige Wellington by attacking him in a position of his own choosing, but after some skirmishing and the capture of two unimportant hamlets outside the Allied line, the French army halted. For two days the armies faced each other within cannon-shot. Then the French withdrew.

Many thought that, while Marmont hesitated, Wellington should have attacked. He had numerical superiority in both infantry and cavalry and the enemy had a long stretch of open plain to his rear. The Allied commander considered the idea and discarded it. 'Between the 20th and the 22nd, I had a favourable opportunity of attacking the enemy, of which, however, I did not think it proper to avail myself for the following reasons. First, it was probable he had advanced with an intention to attack us, and in the position which we occupied, I considered it advantageous to be attacked; and that the action would be attended with less loss on our side.

'Secondly; the operations against the forts at Salamanca took up the attention of some of our troops; and although I believe the superiority of numbers in the field was on our side, the superiority was not so great as to render an action decisive of the result of the campaign, in which we should sustain great loss.

'Thirdly; in the case of failure, the passages of the Tormes would have been difficult, the enemy continuing in possession of the forts, and commanding the bridge of Salamanca.'

Whatever the rights and wrongs of Wellington's refusal to attack, the impression produced on the mind of Marmont was decisive. He was convinced that Wellington could not, or would not, risk an attacking battle.

Meanwhile the siege of the convents in Salamanca was making poor progress. 'I was mistaken', confessed Wellington, 'in my estimate of the extent of the means which would be necessary to subdue these forts; and I was obliged to send to the rear for a fresh supply of ammunition. This necessitated a delay of six days.' It was not until 27th June that the forts capitulated and Wellington felt free to advance.

By the end of June Marmont was in position behind the Douro with his left on Tordesillas. Here on 7th July, the division from the Asturias joined the army, bringing the infantry strength up to 43,000. Ruthless requisitioning of horses from infantry officers enabled a thousand dragoons from the reinforcement depot at Valladolid to be mounted and the French cavalry brought up to numbers roughly equal to the British.

Marmont's army was now complete, but it was alone. The Army of the North, alarmed at the raids of Home Popham, declined to part with any infantry but, too late, despatched a thousand horsemen and a battery. Joseph in Madrid demanded help from Soult but received a blank refusal. His letters to Marmont had to travel by way of Segovia, taking 12 days even when the guerrillas did not intercept them. The last despatch which Marmont received from the King urged him to give battle in good position but held out no hope of reinforcement.

Wellington had moved his army up to the Douro and had even put some companies across. He, also, was disappointed of support. The Spanish Army of Galicia, relieved of the French presence in the Asturias had undertaken to harass Marmont's rear, but their commander, Santocildes, acted with such extreme caution that the French had no need to acknowledge their existence. Only the Portuguese dragoons covering the militia's investment of Astorga circumscribed the activities of the French foraging parties, and forced Marmont to think of advancing while there was still enough food to support his troops.

On 16th July he feinted to his right, pushing two divisions across the bridge at Toro. This was the move that Wellington had expected, a thrust at his communications with Salamanca. Orders were at once given for five divisions to concentrate westward to meet the threat. But while they were still on the move, Marmont countermarched, crossed at Tordesillas and fell on the Allied reserve, the Fourth and Light Divisions and three regiments of light dragoons at Castrejon. Soon after dawn on the 18th the commander of the Light Division's outlying piquet was amazed when 'Lord Wellington, with his staff, and a cloud of English and French dragoons and horse artillery intermixed, came over the hill at full cry, and all hammering at each other's heads in one confused mass, over the very ground that I had that instant quitted. It appeared that his Lordship had gone there to reconnoitre, covered by two guns and two squadrons of cavalry, who by some accident, were surprised and charged by a superior body of the enemy. We were obliged to remain passive spectators of such an extraordinary scene going on within a few yards of us, as we could not fire without an equal chance of shooting some of our own side. Lord Wellington and his staff, with the two guns, took shelter for the moment behind us, while the cavalry went sweeping along our front, where, I suppose, they picked up some reinforcements for they returned almost instantly, in the same confused mass; but the French were now the flyers; and, I must do them the justice to say that they got themselves off in a manner highly creditable to themselves. Marshal Beresford and the greater part of the staff remained with their swords drawn, and the Duke himself did not look more than half pleased, while he silently despatched some of them with orders.'

By midday, Wellington's reserve, now his rear-guard, was safely in line with the rest of the army behind the Guareña river between Castrillo and Vallesa, and there was no further movement that day.

Throughout the morning of 19th July the two armies faced each other across the Guareña, while the French rested after three days of forced marches, but at mid-afternoon they could be seen marching southward. The Allies at once followed suit and until nightfall the two armies marched in parallel columns, exchanging an occasional round of cannon-fire.

Wellington saw clearly that it was Marmont's aim to put the Army of Portugal across the Allied lines of communication with Portugal and had no option but to conform to their march. He had every reason for caution as he had just learned from a captured despatch that King Joseph had decided to abandon central Spain and march to Marmont's aid with 15,000 men, leaving behind him only garrisons in Madrid and Toledo. The arrival of this corps would give the French a clear superiority in numbers, and it was impossible to be certain that Marmont had not received a duplicate of the despatch.

Next morning the French continued to move southward. The Allies conformed, marching in three parallel columns, ready at any moment to turn left into line and receive an attack. 'Our people much harassed and fatigued, as the heat was incessant, and no water hardly to be found. But I suppose there never was a more interesting or beautiful sight than that of two hostile armies of upwards of 35,000 men each moving parallel within a mile and a half of each other and often within cannon range.'

The French outmarched the Allies and reached Cantalpino first. Rather than fight a general action there, on ground that did not promise a decisive victory, Wellington swung the heads of his columns to the south-west allowing Marmont to reach the Tormes at the fords of Huerta and to take

The Duke of Wellington by Francisco Goya

'A View of the Serra de Busacco at St. Antonio de Cantaro' from an aquatint by C. Turner after a watercolour drawing by Major T. St. Clair

'Bury them and Keep Quiet' from an etching by Francisco Goya

Auguste Marmont,
Duc de Raguse from
an engraving by
J.N. Joly after a
drawing by Meyer

André Massena, Prince
of Essling from a
lithograph by
F.S. Delpech

Sir Thomas Graham by Sir Thomas
Lawrence

Sir William Beresford from an engraving
after a drawing by Carlo Amatucci

Sir Rowland Hill by Thomas Heaphy

up a position from which they could threaten the road from Salamanca to Rodrigo by which Wellington's supplies must come and by which the army must retreat.

On the night of 21st July, both armies lay astride the Tormes close to Salamanca. The French at Huerta, the Allies at Santa Marta. Realising that Marmont had outmanœuvred them and thinking that Wellington would continue to retreat, the British were despondent. 'For days past the enemy appeared to control our movements, and to force us back without an effort; we were now, in the darkness of the night, close to him – but where, or in what direction, was known only to the headquarters.' To make matters worse, the elements seemed to have turned against them. 'Before reaching our ground, we experienced one of the most tremendous thunderstorms I have ever witnessed. A sheet of lightning struck the head of our column, where I happened to be riding, and deprived me of the use of my optics for at least ten minutes. A great many of our dragoon horses broke from their piqueting during the storm, and galloped past us into the French lines. We lay on our arms on the bank of the river, and it continued to rain in torrents the whole of the night.'

Marmont was full of confidence. He thought he could drive his opponent back into Portugal and he was certain that Wellington would not attack him. He hoped that if he continued moving round the Allies' right flank they would allow themselves to be shepherded away. His intention was to 'press near enough to him to be able to profit from the first fault he might make, and to attack him with full vigour. . . . I considered that our respective positions would not bring on a battle, but an advantageous rear-guard action, in which, using my full force late in the day, with a part only of the British army left in front of me, I should probably score a point.' His army was almost 48,000 strong, including eight infantry divisions, 3,400 cavalry and 78 guns. He was expecting soon to be joined by the brigade of cavalry from the Army of the North which was at last approaching, but he knew nothing of the help promised to him by King Joseph.

On the Allied side, Wellington had slightly augmented his numbers. A weak brigade of Portuguese dragoons had joined him from the north bank of the Douro and two battalions of newly arrived British infantry had arrived from Lisbon. These additions brought the Allied strength up to 51,000. This small superiority in numbers was more than offset by the variable fighting qualities of the nationalities which made up the Allied army. While Marmont's force was, except for a remnant of 80 Prussians, wholly French, Wellington's army was made up of 24,000 British, 5,000 Germans, 18,000 Portuguese, 3,300 Spaniards and 1,700 *émigré* French.

In cavalry he outnumbered his adversary by a thousand sabres but he had 24 fewer guns. He was also without two of his best generals, as Graham had been forced to return to England with serious eye-trouble and Picton, whose Badajoz wound had broken out again, had left the command of the Third Division in the hands of Edward Pakenham, Wellington's brother-in-law.

Knowing the strength of the reinforcement that was soon to join Marmont, Wellington could not afford to be other than cautious. On the night of 21st July, he wrote: 'I have determined to cross the Tormes, if the enemy should; to cover Salamanca as long as I can; and above all, not to give up our communication with Ciudad Rodrigo; and not to fight an action, unless under very advantageous circumstances, or if it should become absolutely necessary.'

6

Salamanca – 22nd July 1812

Morning found the Allied army in position to cover Salamanca, drawn up along a ridge perpendicular to the south bank of the Tormes. On the extreme left, the Third Division with d'Urban's Portuguese cavalry brigade were still holding a bridge-head on the north bank of the river. Before dawn the Fourth Division occupied a flat-topped hill, the Arapil Chico, at which the ridge swung through a right angle and continued westwards towards the Ciudad Rodrigo road. A thousand yards to the southward of this point stood another similar height, longer and a few feet higher, the Arapil Grande, but in the half-light it seemed far away and less dominating, and neither the divisional commander, Lowry Cole, nor Wellington appreciated its importance.

The ground here consists of two L-shaped ridges lying one inside the other. At the angle are the two Arapils. The Arapil Chico is attached to the angle of the inner, or British ridge; the Arapil Grande is freestanding but close to the outer, or French ridge.

In front of the Allies as they faced east was the dry bed of the Algabete stream, and piquets of the Seventh Division, supported by cavalry, were holding the chapel of Nuestra Señora de la Pena on a slight rise on the east bank. It was here that the first shots of the day were fired. French cavalry scouts, pushing forward from the fords of Huerta, reached Calvarrasa de Arriba at dawn. Foy's division of infantry was close behind, and Marmont rode with them. Immediately, the Marshal ordered an attack on the chapel and the piquet was driven back. Wellington reacted strongly and sent two battalions to take and hold the mound. This they did without difficulty. The chapel remained all day in British hands, although skirmishing around the knoll continued for many hours.

While this bickering was in progress, a further French division, Bonnet's, began to march towards the Arapil Grande. Told of this belatedly, Wellington ordered the *caçadore* battalion of the Fourth Division to make a dash for the height. Both forces broke into a double, but the French gained the crest by a short head and drove the *caçadores* back in some disorder. Possession of the higher of the two Arapils gave the French a firm base from which to strike at the road to Portugal. For a time Wellington considered ordering a counter-attack. The First

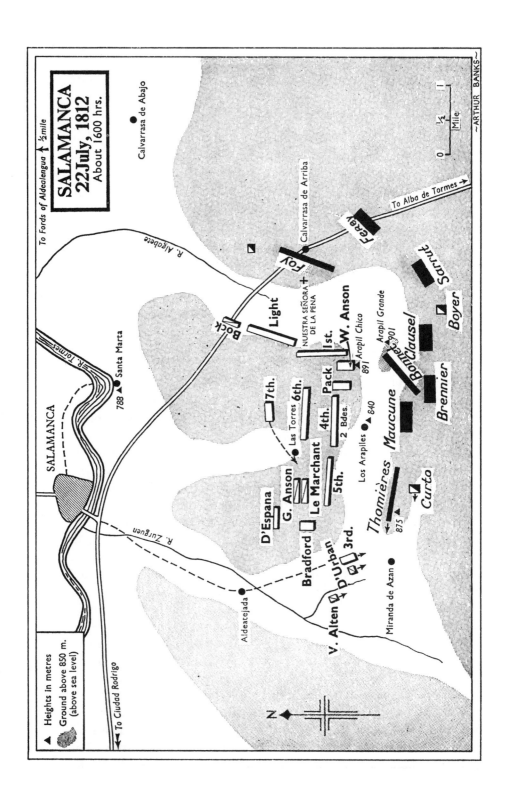

SALAMANCA
22 July, 1812
About 1600 hrs.

To Aldealengua ↑ ½mile

To Fords of Aldealengua

Calvarrasa de Abajo

R. Aregbete

Calvarrasa de Arriba

To Alba de Tormes →

Foy

Feey

Sarrut

Boyer

Light

NUESTRA SEÑORA
DE LA PENA

W. Anson

Arapil Grande

BonTee Clausel

901

Bock

1st.

Arapil Chico

891

Brennier

R. Tormes

Santa Marta

788

Pack

4th.

2 Bdes.

840

Maucune

SALAMANCA

7th.

6th.

Las Torres

Curto

Los Arapiles

Thomières

875

R. Zurguen

G. Anson

Le Marchant

5th.

D'Espana

Bradford

D'Urban

3rd.

Miranda de Azan

V. Alten

Aldeatejada

To Ciudad Rodrigo

N

Heights In metres

▲ Ground above 850 m.
(above sea level)

0   ½   1
Mile

~ARTHUR BANKS~

Division was called forward, but, on Beresford's advice, the order was countermanded and the staff was told to prepare orders for the retreat of the whole army behind the Zurguen stream. To cover this move the Third Division with the Portuguese dragoons marched through Salamanca and took up a position on the west bank of the Zurguen near Aldeatejada. Much of the rest of the army was also moved westward, the Fifth and Sixth Divisions with Bradford's Portuguese brigade, Don Carlos' Spaniards and three British cavalry brigades moving to Las Torres, an area hidden from the French by the intervening ridge. The Allied army now covered the angle of the ridge. Facing east were the Light, First and Seventh, flanked by two cavalry brigades. Anson's brigade of the Fourth Division held the Arapil Chico, while the remainder of that division, extended by Pack's Portuguese brigade, were in line along the westward ridge, with, at the foot of the slope, the light companies of the Guards holding the village of Arapiles. The Third Division were on the march from Santa Marta to Aldeatejada, and the bulk of the reserves at Las Torres. The morning passed with continued skirmishing around Nuestra Señora de la Pena and occasional cannonading between the Arapils. 'The day was fine the sun shone bright . . . occasional smoke from the firing, and dust, alone created a temporary uncertainty in the view.' Across the valley the French could be seen massing behind the Arapil Grande. Continuing his shift to the right, Wellington ordered the Seventh Division to hand over Nuestra Señora to the Light Division and to join the reserve at Las Torres, while the Fifth Division moved to the flank of the Fourth on the ridge.

On the summit of the Arapil Grande, Marmont was watching the Allied movements. His view was imperfect since most of the troops were in dead ground. He could see a division supporting the skirmishers around Nuestra Señora, and the Fourth Division was clearly visible. He had also seen the threatening advance of the First Division and its countermarch. This confirmed him in his belief that Wellington would not attack. Away to the west, clouds of dust showed that a large-scale movement was in progress. It was the baggage of the Allied army, sent off at dawn towards Rodrigo under escort of a single regiment of Portuguese dragoons. Marmont took it to be the bulk of the Allied army. Now was the time for the 'advantageous rear-guard action' for which he had hoped.

Soon after midday Marmont pushed out Maucune's division to his left. It moved along the ridge until it had passed the village of Arapiles and halted facing the Fifth Division, sending skirmishers down into the valley. General Leith, considering that 'this column had every appearance of meditating an immediate attack' ordered his aide-de-camp, [Captain

Leith Hay] 'to proceed as expeditiously as possible . . . to inform Lord Wellington of this demonstration. On being made acquainted with the posture of affairs, he announced his intention of riding to the spot, and directed me to accompany him. When he arrived at the ground of 5th Division, now under arms and perfectly prepared to receive the attack, his Lordship found the enemy in the same formation as when he first appeared opposite, but not displaying any intention of trying his fortune by crossing the ravine at that point.' The French had brought up 20 guns but Wellington, convinced that this was not to be a serious attack, ordered the Fifth Division to fall back over the crest of the ridge, out of the line of fire and rode to the right flank of the army.

It was now after three o'clock, and although *voltigeurs* were skirmishing with the Guards in Arapiles village, there was no sign of a general action. Marmont had only three divisions in line. One on the Arapil Grande, one to the south, opposite Nuestra Señora and the third opposite the Fifth Division. Two reserve divisions, those of Ferey and Sarrut, supported Foy to the north-east of the Arapil and the remaining three, those of Clausel, Thomières and Brennier, were in the woods to the south of that height.

About four o'clock, 'Lord Wellington. . . sat down to eat a few mouthfuls of cold beef. He had scarcely commenced when his aide-de-camp said, "the enemy are in motion, my Lord!" "Very well; observe what they are doing" was the reply. A minute or so elapsed, when the aide-de-camp said, "I think they are extending to the left". "The devil they are!" said his Lordship, springing upon his feet, – "give me the glass quickly". He took it, and for a short space continued observing the motions of the enemy with earnest attention. "Come!" he exclaimed, "I think this will do at last",' and he galloped to his right towards Aldeatejada.

Still convinced that he had only a strong rear-guard to his front, Marmont had decided to extend his left still further. Thomières was to move to the left of Maucune, while Brennier acted as a support to them both. Thomières marched off very rapidly, opening a gap between his right and the left to Maucune's division. It was this gap that had shown Wellington his opportunity. Arriving at Aldeatejada 'at a rapid gallop accompanied only by Col. Delancey',* he gave his orders first to d'Urban and then to Pakenham. In the Third Division, 'the soldiers had but just resumed their arms when Lord Wellington appeared amongst them. The officers had not taken their places in the column, but were in a group

---

* Acting Quartermaster-General.

together in front of it . . . . He looked paler than usual but he was quite unruffled, and as calm as if the battle to be fought was nothing more than an ordinary assemblage of troops for a field-day. His words were few, and his orders brief. Tapping Pakenham on the shoulder, he said, "Edward, move on with the Third Division – take that hill to your front – and drive everything before you." "I will, my Lord," was the laconic reply of the gallant Sir Edward.'

Pakenham, with his supporting dragoons, had 5,000 yards to cover to head off Thomières' march to the end of the ridge above Miranda de Azan. Almost the whole of the route lay in dead ground. As the Third Division marched off in two columns of lines, with the cavalry on the right flank, Wellington galloped back to the crest of the ridge above the village of Arapiles. There he gave orders for a far more powerful attack. The Fifth and Fourth Divisions were to storm the ridge to their front, the Seventh and Sixth Divisions were to advance in second line and the two independent Portuguese brigades were to cover the flanks, Pack on the left of the Fourth and Bradford on the right of the Fifth. The cavalry was to support the open right flank, except for one light brigade which was to reinforce d'Urban on the extreme right.

About this time Marmont began to be concerned about the gap which separated Thomières from Maucune, a gap that Brennier had done nothing to fill, having drawn up his division in rear of that of Maucune. He determined to ride down from the Arapil Grande and to order Brennier forward. As he mounted his horse a shell burst beside him gravely damaging his right arm, which later had to be amputated, and breaking two ribs. Command passed to the senior divisional commander, Bonnet, who was on the Arapil, but before many minutes had passed he too was a casualty, and it was some time before the next senior general, Clausel, could be informed and before he could take over control.

On the extreme right, above Miranda de Azan, d'Urban was first into action. Thomières was advancing in battalion columns, without much co-ordination. He had no skirmishers to his front and Curto's division of dragoons which accompanied him was riding on the southern side of the ridge. The first intimation that the French had of danger was when d'Urban at the head of the 1st Portuguese Dragoons charged into the leading French battalion and scattered them. Hardly had the battalion broken, when the Third Division came into sight on the right front. A flat space, a thousand yards in breadth, had to be crossed before Pakenham could reach the heights. The French batteries opened a heavy fire, to which two brigades of artillery, commanded by Captain Douglas, posted on rising ground behind the Third Division replied.

'Wallace's three regiments* advanced in open column until two hundred and fifty yards of the ridge held by the French infantry. Pakenham, who was naturally of a boiling spirit and hasty temper, was on this day perfectly cool. He told Wallace to form line from open column without halting, and thus the different companies, by throwing forward their right shoulders were in line without the slow movement of a deployment.

'In spite of the fire of Thomières' *tirailleurs* they [Pakenham and Wallace] continued at the head of the right brigade, while the soldiers, with their firelocks at rest, followed close. They speedily got footing upon the brow of the hill, but before they had time to take breath, Thomières' entire division, with drums beating and uttering loud shouts, ran forward to meet them, and belching forth a torrent of bullets, brought down almost the entire of Wallace's first rank, and more than half of his officers. The brigade staggered back from the force of the shock, but before the smoke had altogether cleared away, Wallace looking full in the faces of his soldiers, pointed to the French column, and leading the shattered brigade up the hill, brought them face to face before the French had time to witness the terrible effect of their murderous fire.

'Astounded by the unshaken determination of Wallace's soldiers, Thomières' division wavered: nevertheless they opened a heavy discharge of musketry, but it was unlike the former – it was irregular and ill-directed, the men acted without concert or method, and many fired in the air. At length their fire ceased altogether, and the three regiments, for the first time, cheered. The effect was electric; the French troops were seized with a panic . . . Pakenham, seeing that the proper moment had come, called out to Wallace "to let them loose".'

As the Third Division went in with the bayonet, driving the broken division before them, a brigade of Curto's French dragoons at last appeared on the scene. They charged in from the dense smoke on the flanking battalions of the two leading brigades. In the front line, the 45th drove them off without difficulty, but the 5th in their rear were thrown into some confusion. 'We retired, slowly, in good order, not far, not a hundred paces; General Pakenham approached, and very good naturedly said "reform" and in about a moment, "advance", adding, "there they are, my lads, just let them feel the temper of your bayonets". We advanced, everyone making up his mind for mischief.'

The dragoons, blasted by musketry, were driven off by the 1st Hussars of the Legion and the 14th Light Dragoons, and all organised French

---

* 1/45th, 74th, 1/88th.

opposition in this part of the field collapsed. Thomières' division was finished as a fighting formation. Thomières himself was killed, an eagle and six guns were captured; 2,130 men out of the 4,500 were casualties, the bulk of the loss falling on the two leading regiments, which together lost 1,899 casualties out of a strength of 2,572. The survivors streamed back into Maucune's division, arriving just as it was bracing itself to meet the shock of Wellington's main attack.

The main blow had been somewhat delayed while Bradford's brigade came forward from Las Torres to take its place on the right of the Fifth Division. Meanwhile, under heavy cannon fire 'General Leith, on horseback, passed repeatedly along the front of his division, speaking to and animating the men, who earnestly expressed an anxious desire to attack the enemy.

'At last the welcome intelligence was imparted that we were no longer to be cannonaded with impunity. General Leith was directed to form his division in two lines, the first of which was composed of the Royal, 9th, and 38th regiments, with part of the 4th regiment from General Pringle's brigade, necessarily brought forward for the purpose of equalising the lines, of which the second was formed by the remainder of General Pringle's and the whole of General Spry's Portuguese infantry.

'When General Bradford's brigade came up, the division was to . . . march directly up the heights, and attack the enemy's column. Lord Wellington on this, as on all other occasions, gave his orders in a clear, concise and spirited manner; there was no appearance of contemplating a doubtful result; all he directed was as to time and formation, and his instructions that the enemy should be overthrown and driven from the field. He then proceded towards the 4th division. The 5th formed as he had directed, with its general in front of the centre of the line, impatiently awaiting the arrival of General Bradford; the moment he was in line, General Leith gave the signal, and the whole advanced in the most perfect order. Previously he had despatched his aides de camp, Captain Belcher and Captain Dowson, to different parts of the line, in order to restrain any effort at getting more rapidly forward than was consistent with the important object of its arriving in perfect order close to the enemy, and at all points making a simultaneous attack. In ascending the height on which the French army was placed, the division continued to be annoyed by the artillery fire from its summit; the ground between the advancing force and that to be assailed was also crowded with light troops in extended order, carrying on a very incessant tiraillade. The general desired me to ride forward, make the light infantry press up the heights to clear his line of march, and if practicable make a rush at the enemy's cannon. The light troops soon drove back those opposed; the cannon were removed to the rear; every obstruction to the regular advance of the line had vanished. In front of the centre of that beautiful line rode General Leith, directing its movements, and regulating its advance. Occasionally every soldier was visible, the sun shining brightly on their arms, while at intervals all were enveloped in a dense cloud of dust.'

The enemy, 'his columns, retired from the crest of the height, were formed in squares, about fifty yards removed from the ground, on which, when arrived, the British regiments would become visible. The French artillery, although placed more to the rear, still poured its fire on the advancing troops.

'The second line of the division was about a hundred yards in rear of the first. No advance in line at a review was ever more correctly executed; the dressing was admirable, and spaces no sooner formed by casualties than closed up with perfect regularity.'

Maucune's division 'was drawn up in contiguous squares, the front rank kneeling, and prepared to fire when the drum beat for its commencement. All was quiet and still in these squares; not a musket was discharged until the whole opened. General Leith ordered the line to fire and charge: the roll of musketry was succeeded by that proud cheer. Every individual present was enveloped in smoke and obscurity. No struggle for ascendancy took place: the French squares were penetrated, broken and discomforted.'

As Maucune's men broke and ran for the shelter of Brennier's division in the rear, the British heavy cavalry burst in on their left flank. Wellington had ridden forward between the two lines of the Fifth Division and as the French squares broke he ordered Le Marchant to 'charge in at all hazards'. Le Marchant, until a few months previously the first Lieutenant-Governor and Superintendent-General of the Royal Military College, wheeled his three regiments into line and plunged into the flying French. With the 5th Dragoon Guards and the 4th Dragoons in first line and the 3rd Dragoons in reserve, the horsemen made a terrible slaughter with their heavy sabres amongst the disorganised and defenceless infantry, many of whom threw down their arms and called for quarter. Leaving them to be collected by the Fifth Division, the dragoons reformed and charged at Maucune's reserve brigade, breaking it though not without heavy loss to themselves.

'The nature of the ground, which was an open wood of evergreen oaks, and which grew more obstructed as they advanced, had caused the men of the three regiments to become a good deal mixed in each other's ranks; and the front being at the same time constantly changing as the right was brought forward, the whole had now crowded into a solid line, without any intervals.' Nevertheless seeing another body of French infantry to his front Le Marchant again ordered the dragoons to charge. This was the leading brigade of Brennier's division, who 'taking advantage of the trees, had formed a *colonne serrée*, and stood awaiting their charge. These men reserved their fire with much coolness, till the cavalry came within twenty yards, when they poured it into the concentrated mass of men and horses with a deadly and tremendous effect.' The gallant General Le Marchant, with Captain White of his staff, were killed; and it is thought that nearly one-third of the dragoons came to the ground; but as the remainder retained sufficient command of their horses to dash forward, they succeeded in breaking the French ranks, and dispersing them in utter confusion over the field. 'By this time, (about 40 minutes after the first charge, which took place soon after five o'clock,) it was with difficulty that three squadrons could be collected and formed out of the whole brigade.'

The heavy dragoon brigade, although its casualties were little more than one hundred out of the thousand that had taken part in the first charge, was now a spent force. It had consolidated the victory on the right to such an extent that with the divisions of Thomières and Maucune broken and Brennier's seriously damaged, more than a quarter of the French infantry was out of the fight. On the southern ridge, formerly held by three French divisions, the Third and Fifth Divisions were now joining hands and reforming ready to sweep eastward on the flank of the remainder of the French infantry.

On the left of the Fifth Division the situation was less satisfactory. The Fourth Division started its advance somewhat later than the Fifth as their forming-up ground was more difficult. 'The line of the division went through the village of Arapiles by files from the right of companies, covered by the light troops; and when through, the companies formed up upon their Sergeants regularly sent out, under a heavy fire from the enemy's guns.'

Having left Anson's brigade on the Arapil Chico, the two remaining brigades were formed in a single line with the Fusilier brigade on the right and Power's Portuguese brigade on the left. As the division advanced the Portuguese began to suffer increasingly from the fire of the French on the Arapil Grande and Cole, worried lest his left should be attacked, deployed his *caçadore* battalion on that side. Wellington had assigned responsibility for this flank to the Portuguese of Denis Pack, giving him discretion to assault the Arapil if he considered that circumstances made such a move necessary. Pack decided to wait on events and meanwhile formed his brigade 'as if he were storming a fortress. A party of about one hundred men of the 4th Caçadores under Major Fearon were to form the advance, or storming party, and were ordered to gain as much ground up the hill as the enemy would let them. Two companies of Grenadiers of the 16th and two companies of Grenadiers of the 1st were formed as a support to the storming party, and the command given to Sir Neil Campbell. The remainder of the 4th Caçadores were to steal up the sides of the hill and cover themselves as best they could. Sir Neil Campbell's four hundred Grenadiers were in line; in rear of his right were the 1st Regiment, while in rear of his left in column was the 16th.'

The brigade lay down and watched the Fourth Division as they advanced, and soon a message came from Sir Lowry Cole asking for help. Pack thereupon decided to storm the Arapil Grande. At the last moment he divided his storming party into two with Fearon commanding one half and his aide-de-camp, Captain Synge, in charge of the other. 'Sir Denis Pack had ordered that none should load, but that the Hill should be carried with the bayonet (knowing well that if such troops as we had began firing we should never get to the top).

'The roar of the enemy's guns was tremendous as we approached the top, and somewhat unusual in its sound, for they tried to depress the muzzle as much as possible, and though they could not do so much harm, it sounded as if they all but touched the top of our heads. The last part of the ascent was so steep that it was all but impossible for a horse to climb it; even the men did so with difficulty. It was not until we were close to the summit that I knew what we had to contend with, for I found the ground, which had at a little distance the appearance of a gentle slope, formed a natural wall of, I suppose, between three and four feet high, at the top of which it spread out into a level table-land, on which the enemy were drawn up in line about ten yards from me. We looked at each other for a moment. I saw immediately that what we had undertaken was impractical, as the men could not mount the scarped ground without first laying their arms on the top, and even then in such small numbers that it would be absurd – but I also saw that we were so easily covered by "the wall", and the enemy so exposed from head to foot, that if we fired they could not remain an instant. At this critical instant, the head of Sir Noel Hill's column [1st Portuguese line regiment], which had followed me in support, was close up, and Hill called to me to ask what to do and what was before us (he could not see). I said, "Be quick and let your leading company close up to this bank and fire away while the others deploy as fast as they can and fire as they get up – the enemy are exposed and we are protected by this parapet." To my horror Hill replied, "You forget that we are not loaded!" "Well," I said, "we have no other chance. Load away as fast as you can." He gave the order, and the men were in the act, and two or three of the storming party were trying to scramble up the scarp, when the whole line opposed to us fired, knocked me over, and literally cut to pieces the few that had climbed the wall.

'The French line followed up their volley by charging up to the end of the scarp, down which they leapt when they saw our confusion. Sir Neil Campbell's Grenadiers, the left column and all went! the disaster was complete.'

The repulse of the Portuguese from the Arapil gave Clausel, now in command on the French side, a last chance to save his army from total disaster. The flank of the Fourth Division was open. He had in hand such of Bonnet's division as was not needed on the Arapil, his own division and Sarrut's, which had been withdrawn from supporting Foy, together with Boyer's division of dragoons. Leaving Sarrut to ward off the Third and Fifth Divisions, Clausel threw the remainder on to Cole's open flank.

The Fusilier brigade had just reached the crest of the ridge driving their opponents before them when the French counter-attacked with 'a spirited charge of four battalions in column', driving them back into the valley. On their left, the Portuguese were in even worse case. The left-hand battalion of the Portuguese brigade 'struggled gallantly against very superior forces, but it was overwhelmed and broken; and it suffered much from the French cavalry. General Anson had moved by order of Lord Wellington, with the 40th Regiment, to the right of General Pack; and on his attacking the height, had advanced, but was overpowered; and compelled to fall back on his ground in the original position.'

The French success was short-lived. Beresford led the Portuguese brigade from the Fifth Division obliquely on to the flank of their advance, while the Sixth Division swept across the valley to the support of the Fourth. Bonnet's regiments which formed the right of the French counter-attack suffered the worst. The line of the Sixth Division bore down on them, overlapping them at each end. A short but devastating exchange of volleys took place and the French streamed away to the rear leaving 1,500 men on the ground. Their flight left the flank of Clausel's division open. These regiments, with the Sixth Division moving on the right rear and the Fifth assailing their front, broke and fled, as did Sarrut's which had the Third to their front and three brigades of cavalry constantly overlapping their right.

At this stage, Wellington began to wheel up his left. The First Division in line marched round the east side of the Arapil Grande, sending the light companies of the German Legion against the crest. The three battalions which formed the garrison of the hill retired while they still could, leaving six guns.

At the edge of the thick woodland to the south of the Arapil, the Army of Portugal made its last stand. Only Ferey's division was available to stem the overwhelming tide. It was growing dark and, without waiting to reform, Clinton led the Sixth Division straight at them. 'The ground over which we had to pass was a remarkably clear slope, like the glacis of a fortress, most favourable for the defensive fire of the enemy, and disadvantageous for the assailant. The craggy ridge on which the French were drawn up rose so abruptly that the rear ranks could fire over the heads of the front. But we had approached within two hundred yards before the musketry began: it was far the heaviest that I have ever seen, and accompanied by constant discharges of grape. An uninterrupted blaze was thus maintained, so that the crest of the hill seemed one long streak of flame. Our men came down to the charging position, and commenced firing from that level, at the same time keeping touch to the right, so that the gaps opened by the enemy's fire were instantly filled up. At the first volley that we received, about eighty men of the right wing of my regiment fell to the rear in one group; the commanding officer rode up to know the cause, and found that they were all wounded.'

The leading brigades, both British, drove the French back from the crest of the hill, suffering crippling casualties. More than one man in three fell in the six battalions, and in two the proportion was above one in two. They could go no further, and Clinton sent his five Portuguese battalions to try to complete the destruction of Ferey's resolute division, with British brigades from the Fourth and Fifth Divisions in support. 'Formed right up against the trees,' wrote a French officer, 'no longer with any artillery to help, we saw the enemy marching up against us in two lines, the first of which was composed of Portuguese. Our position was critical, but we waited for the shock; the two lines moved up towards us; their order was so regular that in the Portuguese regiment in front of us we could see the company intervals, and note the officers keeping the men in accurate line, by blows with the flat of their swords or their canes. We fired first, the moment they got within range; and the volleys which we delivered from our front two ranks were so heavy and so continuous that, though they tried to give us back fire for fire, the whole melted away. The second line was coming up behind – this was English, we should have tried to receive it in the same way, still holding our ground though under a flank fire of artillery, when suddenly the left of our line ceased firing and fell back into the wood in complete disorder.' Wellington's swinging right had arrived behind Ferey's left and there was nothing more that they could do but retire, which they did in reasonable order.

The ultimate French rear-guard was Foy's division from the extreme right. The Light Division pursued them 'but as they were already in the act of retrograding, nothing more than a sharp fire of Light troops took place'. After dusk the commander of the 43rd was still marching after Foy under a 'Disagreeable fire' when 'the Duke rode up *alone* behind my regiment and I joined him; he was giving me some orders when a ball passed through his left holster and struck his thigh; he put his hand to the place and his countenance changed for an instant but only for an instant; and to my eager inquiry if he was hurt, he replied sharply "No" and went on with his orders'.

The Light Division camped that night by the fords of Huerta. There they should have found the wreck of the French army struggling to cross the Tormes. Only a few stragglers were there. Wellington had seen that when the French retreated they would be hemmed in by the sharp angle of the river. There were only two possible crossing places, the fords of Huerta and the bridge at Alba de Tormes. For some weeks the castle which dominated the bridge had been garrisoned by 2,000 Spaniards from the division of Don Carlos de España. 'Before the action Don Carlos asked if he should not take his troops out of Alba – after he had done it – hoping for an order. Lord Wellington said "Certainly not"; and the Don was afraid to tell him what he had done. Lord W. acted of course as if it was in our possession.' Thus, while Wellington directed his retreat to Huerta, the French were escaping unmolested by the bridge at Alba.

Without this unfortunate defection few of the French could have escaped. As it was their losses were sufficiently formidable. Although an accurate return was never prepared, the casualties must have exceeded 14,000. Marmont reported to Napoleon that his losses were only 6,000 men and nine guns, but since 7,000 prisoners and 20 guns remained in British hands his estimate can be discounted. Two divisional commanders, Thomières and Ferey were killed, Marmont and Bonnet were both severely wounded. Two eagles were lost. Only one division was in condition to fight when it left the field and that one, Foy's, was soon brought into line with its fellows. On the following day, the Allied advance-guard, led by two brigades of cavalry came up with Foy at Garcia Hernandez. The French cavalry covering the infantry fled before a charge from two squadrons from the 11th and 16th Light Dragoons, leaving the infantry to its fate. The 1st Regiment of Heavy Dragoons of the King's German Legion then charged straight at a battalion of French infantry regularly formed in square and ready to receive it. A volley from the French brought down many of the dragoons but as they surged up to the square a shot brought down a horse across the bayonets of the defenders. Immediately a number of dragoons leapt over the struggling mass of horse and men and broke the square from the inside. A whole battalion surrendered. Encouraged by this success, the 2nd Dragoon Regiment rode at another battalion square and broke that also. A third attempt failed, but the French lost 1,100 men against a loss of only 127 to the dragoons.

The Army of Portugal, now covered by the long-awaited cavalry brigade from the Army of the North streamed away eastward, useless as a fighting force. Wellington did little more than shepherd it away. A full-scale pursuit with his exhausted men and horses would have cost him heavy losses and he could not afford to risk his army against the Army of the North with such remnants as might be battle-worthy of Marmont's force. Nor could he leave his communications open to the Armies of the Centre and the South. In the two days' fighting he had lost almost 5,000, more than 3,000 of them from his British and Germans. Two thousand five hundred of these casualties had fallen on the Fourth and Sixth Divisions and a thousand more had fallen on the Third and Fifth. Only the First, Seventh and Light Divisions were fresh and almost unharmed. The Allies' losses in senior officers were particularly heavy. Beresford was seriously wounded, as were the commanders of the Fourth and Fifth Divisions, while Charles Alten of the Light was slightly injured. In the cavalry, Le Marchant was dead and Victor Alten had a ball in the knee. Stapleton Cotton, the cavalry commander, was shot through the arm on the night following the battle by a Portuguese sentry whose challenge he did not answer. Two Portuguese brigade commanders were also wounded, one of them mortally. With Graham and Picton already away from the army, the lack of senior commanders must have been a potent factor in deciding Wellington not to press the pursuit too far.

Marmont, who returned to France in pain and disgrace, had learned from Masséna's experience that it was unwise to attack Wellington in a position of his own choosing. Twice, in September 1811 and in June 1812 he had had the opportunity for such an assault and had declined it. He had not learned from Soult's experience at Oporto in 1809 that his opponent could, given an opening, attack. When he had trailed his coat with impunity in front of the heights of San Cristobal in June, Marmont concluded that he was for all time safe from attack. This is the only explanation of his conduct on 22nd July. He claimed that it was not in accordance with his orders that Maucune sent his skirmishers down the slope towards Arapiles and menaced the Fifth Division with a major assault, or that Thomières should extend the front so far to the left. It was, he claimed, to stop these movements that he was mounting his horse on the Arapil Grande when he was hit. But either of these orders could more easily have been carried by an aide-de-camp, there was no call for the commander of the whole army to descend from a splendid position of observation to do the work of a captain on the staff. It seems far more probable that his intention was to direct the divisions of Thomières, Maucune and Brennier to strike in between the Arapil Chico and the line of the Zurguen stream. He had retained three divisions to the north-east of the Arapil Grande ready to push westward and had the remaining two on and behind the Arapil to act as a link between the two groups. Being convinced that he had only a rear-guard of two or three divisions before him he may well have hoped with a powerful pincer action to cut the rear-guard off from the main body. An 'advantageous rear-guard action' was his declared aim.

He was supremely confident of his ability to out-manœuvre Wellington. He had reason to be. Twice, at El Bodon and on the Douro, he had completely outwitted him and he thought he could do so again. His over-confidence led him to culpable carelessness. At the moment that Wellington seized his opportunity the French army was in an arc more than six miles long with little communication between the divisions. Thus Wellington was able to attack and break the French divisions piecemeal before their reserves could arrive.

The campaigns against Marmont immeasurably strengthened Wellington's position. After Salamanca his very presence on the battlefield lowered the French morale. One French general confided to his diary that it raised him 'almost to the level of Marlborough'. At home the victory consolidated the new ministry under Liverpool and induced them to reinforce the Peninsular army although they had a new war on their hands in America. Even the opposition in Parliament which for years had railed against the war in the Peninsula as a costly adventure which could only end in humiliating disaster, began bitterly to accuse the Government of neglecting Wellington's army.

PART THREE

Wellington and King Joseph

7

Madrid

Two days after the battle of Salamanca, King Joseph with 14,000 men of the Army of the Centre reached Blasco Sancho on the north side of the Sierra de Guadarrama. Unknown to him the wreck of the Army of Portugal lay that night at Arevalo, less than 15 miles to the north. The following day letters from Clausel and the wounded Marmont gave the first definite news of the battle. Marmont described a temporary reverse, counted his casualties as no more than 5,000 and greatly inflated those of his opponent.* Clausel gave the true picture, said that his men were in no condition for any active operations, discounted the usefulness of any junction with the king, (of whose proximity he was unaware) and made it plain that his only purpose was to fall back on his base at Valladolid. By the time that Joseph received this letter, the Army of Portugal was on its way north at the best speed it could manage, marking its path with an orgy of plunder and indiscipline. Joseph, still hoping that some form of co-operation might be possible, retired westward, keeping to the north side of the Guardarramas, and spent five nights at Segovia before he decided to return to Madrid, where he arrived on 5th August.

The Allied army pursued Clausel at a leisurely pace and entered Valladolid on 30th July, the French retiring towards Burgos with the bulk of their stores, although they left behind 17 guns and 800 men in hospital. Wellington then halted, set up his headquarters at Cuellar and took stock of the situation. The army was exhausted by the marches of the past seven weeks and had outrun its supplies. Many of the battalions, from their losses at Cuidad Rodrigo, Badajos and Salamanca were very low in numbers, the 61st in Sixth Division had fewer than 200 all ranks, and the second battalion 44th, from Leith's division, only 220. Almost more serious was the lack of senior commanders. Only the Sixth and Seventh Divisions were under their regular commanders, Beresford was in hospital, and in the cavalry the senior brigade commander left with the army was so short-sighted that at Garcia Hernandez, when ordered to

---

* In his despatch to Napoleon, Marmont gave his casualties as 6,000, but declared only 5,000 to King Joseph. Neither figure bore any relation to the truth.

charge, he had been forced to request an artillery officer to 'be good enough to show us the way'.

The most tempting course would be to continue the pursuit of Clausel, harrying him until his army finally disintegrated. Such a move would be most exhausting to the troops and would leave an ever-lengthening line of communications open to a blow from the south. Wellington knew that King Joseph had been ordering Soult to detach large bodies of his troops to strengthen the Army of the Centre. On 29th July Joseph had ordered the evacuation of Andalusia and the concentration of the Army of the South at Toledo and it was scarcely conceivable that the Duke of Dalmatia would refuse to obey such an order. The junction of the Armies of the Centre and South in Castile would mean that more than 70,000 men could reach Rodrigo sooner than Wellington even had he pursued Clausel no further than Burgos. He decided, therefore, to take the bulk of the army to Madrid and to leave the task of watching the Army of Portugal to General Clinton with the much depleted Sixth Division, reinforced with five newly arrived but sickly British battalions, a British cavalry brigade, and two weak Spanish divisions from the Army of Galicia.

Apart from one unfortunate incident, the march to Madrid was a triumphal affair. The troops 'were enthusiastically welcomed as they passed through the different towns and villages. . . the inhabitants flocking in vast numbers with a supply of wine, fruit, bread and vegetables which were all bought up by the soldiers; at the termination of the day's march, our bivouacks, or the villages we occupied, were crowded with Spanish girls and young men, who either brought wine, lemonade or fruit; the evening wound up with boleros and fandangos'.

The French retired before them. Only once, a few miles from Madrid, was there any contact between the armies. Late in the afternoon of 11th August a division of French cavalry turned on the Portuguese dragoons who formed the Allied vanguard. The Portuguese advanced to check the leading squadrons, but, as their commander wrote, 'the same men who at Salamanca had followed me into the French ranks like British dragoons, on this 11th of August at the first charge went just far enough to leave me in the midst of the enemy's ranks'. Three guns were temporarily lost and the French crashed in on the second brigade in the Allied order of march, the German dragoons, who were taking up their billets for the night. Only the arrival of the leading infantry forced the French to retire, having inflicted 200 casualties.

King Joseph, with a vast convoy of French and Spanish refugees evacuated Madrid, moving due south, leaving behind a garrison of 2,000 men in an inadequate stronghold, the Retiro. Wellington entered the city in triumph on 12th August. 'Old and young men, women and children, in tens of thousands, kissing the colours of the regiments and the happy ensigns who carried them. They cried, laughed, sung, and danced with joy, so that it was impossible to doubt their sincerity. Few of us were ever so carressed before and most undoubtedly never will be again. The windows and balconies were crowded with elegantly dressed females, all joining in the enthusiasm of the moment.' The garrison surrendered after a token resistance, leaving the Allies a vast haul of military stores and two eagles. Wellington reported soberly, 'It is impossible to describe the joy manifested by the inhabitants of Madrid upon our arrival; and I hope that the prevalence of the same sentiments of detestation of the French yoke, and of a strong desire to secure the independence of their country, which first induced them to set the example of resistance to the usurper, will induce them again to make exertions in the cause of their country, which being more wisely directed, will be more efficacious than those formerly made'.

There was no sign of the expected threat from the south. Soult was so comfortable in his Andalusian vice-royalty that he wasted weeks in pressing on Joseph a specious plan for concentrating the Armies of the South and Centre around Seville, to throw over all communications with France and to leave the Army of Portugal to its own devices. It was not until 24th August that Soult finally, and with the worst possible grace, consented to obey his orders and raise the siege of Cadiz. Even then he marched not on Toledo as he had been ordered but on Valencia, and at no great speed.

While all was quiet to the south, the Army of Portugal was showing unexpected signs of life. Finding his retreat from Valladolid unmolested, Clausel turned about with the more serviceable part of his force and reoccupied that city on 14th August. The Galicians, in whose charge Valladolid was, made no resistance and abandoned to the French 400 wounded prisoners and a large supply of small arms. Foy's division then made a brisk raid along the north bank of the Douro and rescued the garrisons of Toro and Zamora before returning to the main body of the army, on 28th August. To prevent a recurrence of such a nuisance Wellington decided to put the time given to him by Soult's insubordination to good use. Leaving his best troops around Madrid to watch the southern approaches and to have a well-earned rest, he marched north with the First, Fifth and Seventh Divisions to join Clinton's force south of the Douro. He intended to deal Clausel such a blow that he would be free to use his entire force against Joseph and Soult when at last they combined.

For the rest of the campaign Wellington's luck and, seemingly, much of his skill deserted him. He drove Clausel back steadily but without determination and never attempted to force a battle. On 18th September the Allies reached Burgos and their advance came to a halt. The following day the First Division invested the castle and the northern part of the army settled down to await the outcome of the siege.

In mid-October Burgos was still defiant and by that time the concentration of the French armies was complete. Wellington was forced to retreat. The operations of the siege were the most unfortunate that he ever undertook. His siege-train, three 18-pounders, was quite inadequate and the provision of trained engineers, five officers and eight other ranks, ludicrous. Worst of all was Wellington's attitude to the operation. He appears never to have been whole-hearted in his determination to capture the place. Not only did he refuse two practical offers to augment his siege-train, but at each of the three assaults he declined to allow the storming parties to be made strong enough to ensure success. As a result he lost 2,000 men, wasted six weeks, and achieved nothing. On 22nd October the siege was finally raised and the army started a long retreat with 50,000 Frenchmen pressing on their rear-guard. The Army of Portugal, now commanded by General Souham, had been strongly reinforced from the Army of the North and had regained much of its morale, and Wellington with no more than 35,000, of whom one-third were Spaniards, was hard pressed until he reached the Douro at the end of the month. On the other side of Europe, Napoleon abandoned Moscow three days before Wellington left Burgos.

In the first days of October King Joseph and Soult met near Valencia. They mustered between them some 60,000 men without withdrawing any troops from the Armies of Aragon, Valencia and Catalonia, which numbered a further 75,000. Soult's withdrawal from Andalusia had enabled Wellington to bring up Hill's corps from Estremadura with a brigade from the British contingent of the garrison of Cadiz, to the southern wing of his army, but even with these succours the force around Madrid, of which Hill took over the command, was only 36,000 strong, of whom 8,000 were Spaniards. There would have been much more Spanish assistance available had not General Ballasteros, the Captain-General of Andalusia, chosen this moment to refuse to obey orders as a protest against the offer to Wellington by the Cortes of the post of Commander-in-Chief of all the Spanish armies. By 25th August the combined French armies had reached the line of the Tagus and Hill's position was becoming dangerous. He extricated himself with great competence and on 10th November the whole Allied army, numbering 70,000 was drawn up on the strong San Cristobal position covering Salamanca on which Wellington had offered battle to Marmont in the previous June. Like Marmont, Soult declined to be drawn, although when the Armies of Portugal, the Centre and the South were concentrated he had almost 100,000 troops in hand. Instead he preferred to turn the Allied right, only to find that Wellington was facing him on the Arapiles position. He continued to turn the right and this time there could be no repetition of the brilliant stroke of 22nd July. Wellington had no option but to fall back on Portugal.

Although the retreat was only substantially hampered by the French on one day, the damage done to the army was equal to that which a major battle might have done. The weather was abominable. 'The heavy rains had set in, and as the roads in that part of the country cease to be roads for the remainder of the season, we were now walking nearly knee deep, in stiff mud, into which no man could thrust his foot with the certainty of having a shoe at the end of it when he pulled it out again.' To make matters worse the Quartermaster-General who had been forced onto Wellington by the Horse Guards in place of the tried and trusted George Murray, succeeded in sending all the supplies for the army by a divergent route so that no rations reached the troops for the four-day march to Ciudad Rodrigo. Apart from a small number of slaughter cattle which marched with the divisions the only food that the troops could find was acorns. In these conditions the losses through exhaustion and straggling amounted to 5,000 men. It was fortunate that the French were as exhausted and short of provisions as the Allies.

The only day on which the French pressed their pursuit was 17th November when their dragoons got amongst the rear-guard and captured Sir Edward Paget, who had recently joined the army in Graham's place. When the Light Division reached the River Huebra at San Muños they found that the enemy had managed to bring artillery forward on their flank and the rear-guard crossed the river at the double under the fire of 36 guns. Fortunately the shelling had little effect, 'for the ground was a bed of soft mud, in which the shells sank so deep, that in the explosion nothing but clay was thrown up'.

'After dark the commissaries brought up some bullocks for the troops, which were instantly knocked on the head; but it was next to impossible to cook the meat in consequence of the continued rain and sleet, and the green wood not igniting. By dint of perseverance we did at last kindle a spark of a fire and were busily engaged in toasting, on the points of our swords, our scanty rations which had been alive and walking about the forest half an hour before. I shall never forget the dismay and disappointment of some half-dozen of us, when crowded round an apology for a fire, in a state of starvation, and ready to bolt down the beef before it was half toasted, down came the drops of rain from the trees above, shaken violently by the storm, and in an instant extinguished the fire and with it our hopes of a supper. In a fit of despair, we commenced groping about under the trees for acorns, of which consisted our repast; whilst our unfortunate horses plucked away at the leaves, which in reality, was the only food they had had for four days.'

Everyone expected a retreat under further harassing on the following day but at dawn, 'to our delight we saw the French army dismissed, all drying their clothes, and as little in a state to attack as we were desirous of their company. We had a clear, cold, but unmolested march, and fell in with some stores coming.' On 19th November the army was back at its starting point, behind the Agueda.

The morale of the army was at a low ebb. All their victories and sufferings seemed to have brought no advantage. It almost seemed as if the French would never allow them to have a foothold east of Ciudad Rodrigo. Nor were their spirits raised by a confidential circular from their commander, in which he petulantly complained of the indiscipline of the troops on the recent retreat, and which, by some error, was widely publicised. 'The Peer Wellington', wrote William Napier to his wife, 'has just issued a circular to the army, in which he obligingly informs them that they are the greatest knaves and the worst soldiers that he not only ever had to deal with, but worse than any army he ever *read* of. He was good enough to say that he excepted the Light Division and the Guards, but he makes no exceptions in writing.'

Despite the discouraging appearances, the results of the campaign had been enormous. As Wellington reported to London: 'From what I see in the newspapers I am much afraid that the public will be disappointed at the result of the last campaign, notwithstanding that it is in fact the most successful campaign in all its circumstances, and had produced for the cause more important results than any campaign in which a British army has been engaged for the last century. We have taken by siege Ciudad Rodrigo, Badajos, and Salamanca; and the Retiro surrendered. In the mean time the Allies have taken Astorga, Guadalaxara and Consuegra, besides others taken by Duran and Sir H. Popham. In the months elapsed since January this army has sent to England little short of 20,000 prisoners, and they have taken and destroyed or have themselves the use of the enemy's arsenals in Ciudad Rodrigo, Badajos, Salamanca, Valladolid, Madrid, Astorga, Seville, the lines before Cadiz &c; and upon the whole we have taken and destroyed, or we now possess, very little short of 3,000 pieces of cannon. The siege of Cadiz has been raised, and all the countries south of the Tagus have been cleared of the enemy.'

Nor was this all. The whole fiction of Joseph Bonaparte's position as King of Spain had been dealt a blow from which it could never recover. Before Wellington moved another regiment against him, he was forced to move his capital to Valladolid since Madrid was too near the edge of his shrinking realm, while in his rear the Biscayan provinces and Navarre broke out into guerrilla warfare on a scale never before possible.

8

'Farewell Portugal'

Having shepherded Wellington back to the Portuguese frontier, King Joseph set about the forlorn task of re-establishing the French rule in Spain. Andalusia, Estremadura, Murcia, Galicia and the Asturias were gone beyond hope of recall, but he once more set up his capital in Madrid and spread out the Armies of Portugal, the South and the Centre in a great fan from Leon to La Mancha. Knowing that the Allied army was much in need of rest he rightly counted on four or five months of quietness before Wellington could advance. Meanwhile the King's main concern was with his communications with France.

Guerrilla activity in the Biscayan provinces had been much stimulated during the summer of 1812 by the operations of Sir Home Popham and his fleet. When it became necessary to withdraw 10,000 men from the Army of the North to help the Army of Portugal to drive Wellington away from Burgos, the French hold on the mountainous region of Biscay and Navarre became more than precarious. In late November only three ports along the whole north coast of Spain, Santona, Guetaria and San Sebastian, remained in French hands and inland they held no more than a series of fortifications along the main road from Burgos to Bayonne and the fortress of Pamplona. Between these points the guerrilla leaders governed the country in a rough-and-ready fashion, one of them, the great Mina, going so far as to establish customs posts on the French frontier. By the New Year it was clear that General Caffarelli and the 40,000 men of the Army of the North could not cope with the situation. A few towns were retaken but despatches from Paris were still taking four to six weeks to reach Madrid, since to clear the road for a courier meant the mounting of major operations. Joseph wrote continually to Paris soliciting reinforcements and money, but his pleas met with no response. It was not until 6th January that he began to grasp the reason for the delay.

On that day he received from Paris a copy of Napoleon's Bulletin of 3rd December, which gave the first inkling that the Russian campaign had miscarried. Five weeks later he learned of the full extent of the disaster and of the death of the *Grande Armée* in a letter from one of his aides-de-camp who survived the retreat from Moscow. At the same time he received his first orders from his brother. There were to be no reinforcements. Instead, the armies in Spain were to supply drafts and a few complete regiments to help with the reconstitution of the main army. The capital was to be moved to Valladolid and the first priority for operations was to be the subjugation of the northern provinces. Since the Army of the North would probably prove too small for this task, Clausel, who succeeded Caffarelli in command, could call on the Army of Portugal for infantry reinforcements to any extent that he wished. There were, said Napoleon, more than enough men in the Armies of the South and the Centre to fight a defensive campaign against Wellington, whose numbers he reckoned at 30,000 British and 20,000 Portuguese. There was only one crumb of comfort in all this for the unfortunate Joseph. Soult, for whose recall the King had been petitioning for months, was to leave Spain. His place as chief military adviser was to be taken by Jean Baptiste Jourdan, who was already Joseph's Chief of Staff and with whom he was on the best of terms.

Marshal Jourdan was one of the old school of Revolutionary generals. As a youth he had fought under Lafayette in the American War of Independence, but had later left the army to become a pedlar in haberdashery. Re-enlisting after the Revolution he had quickly risen to a general's rank and had become a famous figure in France by commanding the army at the great victory of Fleurus, although there were some who said that this victory was not altogether ascribable to his leadership. It had, however, secured for him the leadership of the famous Army of Sambre-et-Meuse, and his reputation for generalship lasted until he was heavily defeated by the Austrians at Stockach in 1799. From then on he was under a cloud, the more so since he was in opposition to Bonaparte at the *coup d'état* of Brumaire. Out of deference to republican sentiment, he was created a Marshal in 1804, but he never received an Imperial title. He had been sent to Spain as adviser to King Joseph in 1808 but was recalled in disgrace after Talavera and was not employed again until he was asked for by the King when he became titular Commander-in-Chief in the spring of 1812. Jourdan could not be called an outstanding soldier but he was honest and obedient, both rare qualities among the marshals in Spain, and his theoretical appreciations of the situation were often more realistic than those of many more renowned figures including his Imperial master.

Faced with the prospect of having to send 15,000 men back to France and of losing the six infantry divisions of the Army of Portugal to cope with the northern guerrillas, Joseph and Jourdan reorganised their remaining troops to guard against the activities of the Allied army. They were committed to a defensive campaign but they had no clear opinion as to the route by which Wellington might advance. They inclined to the belief that he would again strike up the Salamanca–Valladolid road and decided to meet such a move on the line of the Douro between Toro and Tordesillas, the line on which Marmont had halted Wellington in June 1812. They hoped that on this line the divisions immediately available could stand long enough for the infantry of the Army of Portugal and the two field divisions of the Army of the North to join them and give the King numbers large enough to be able to meet his enemies in the open field. They were, however, worried at the prospect of an Allied advance up the valley of the Tagus, since they knew that Hill's corps was wintering around Alcantara, and to meet this possibility they stationed rather more troops at the southern end of their line than was consistent with the safety of the supposed main axis.

The Army of the South was spread out in a great arc from the Douro to the Tagus, with the flanks at Zamora and Toledo, a division in garrison at Madrid, and a division with a regiment of dragoons at Salamanca. The cavalry of the Army of Portugal, backed by a division seconded from the Army of the Centre, watched the approaches from Galicia, and Joseph had around him at Valladolid the 2,500 men of his Royal Guards, with the remaining division of the Army of the Centre in reserve at Segovia. The nearest infantry division of the Army of Portugal was divided between Palencia and Burgos, two more guarded the main road between Burgos and Bilbao and a fourth was operating on the coast north of that city. The other two divisions were lost in the mountains of Navarre forming part of a flying column with which Clausel was endeavouring, with only moderate success, to hunt Mina.

Troubles were not lacking on the Allied side. As soon as he was certain that the French did not intend to follow him into Portugal, Wellington put the army into winter quarters, leaving a screen of guerrillas and light cavalry to warn him of French movements. Apart from a southerly advanced post at Bejar, the only troops kept forward being the Light Division who, as usual, held the line of the Agueda. The rest of the army was billeted well inside the frontier, but was less dispersed than in previous winters. With Andalusia liberated there was no need for Hill's corps to cover Badajoz and his southern flank was now on the Tagus near Alcantara. The most northerly formation was a brigade of Portuguese dragoons in the mountainous Tras os Montes.

The army's first need was for rest. Not only had 5,000 men been lost in the retreat, but the sick list was enormous. Twenty thousand men were in hospital from the British troops alone and many of the remainder were far from fit.

Despite the demands of war with the United States the Government had contrived to send to Portugal 5,000 men in drafts and five regiments of cavalry giving the British element a held strength of 56 battalions, 18 regiments and 14 batteries. Some of the newly arrived troops were sickly, in particular those which had been on the fever-stricken Walcheren expedition, and the second Guards brigade, which joined the army partly from England and partly from Cadiz was so much beset by dysentery that 700 died and the brigade was not fit for service until August 1813.

Money was another problem. The Spaniards and Portuguese were reluctant to accept paper money and despite its best efforts the Government was quite unable to supply enough coin. A week after Salamanca, Wellington had been forced to write to the Secretary for War: 'We are absolutely bankrupt. The troops are now five months in arrears, instead of being one month in advance. The staff has not been paid since February; the muleteers not since June, 1811; and we are in debt in all parts of the country.'

Nor was Wellington's appointment as Commander-in-Chief of all the Spanish armies much consolation to him. Several Spanish generals already co-operated with him satisfactorily and the rest were unlikely to be both able and willing to do so. As for the troops, 'I am sorry that I cannot say that the Spanish troops are at all improved in their discipline, their equipment, their organisation, or their military spirit.' Worst of all the Spanish supply system was inefficient beyond hope of remedy.

On the command side the picture was a little brighter. Most of the generals who had been wounded at Salamanca rejoined the army, Thomas Graham returned as Second-in-Command and George Murray was allowed to return to his post of Quartermaster-General.

While resolving these problems, Wellington set up his headquarters close behind his forward infantry at Freineda. It was in some ways an inconvenient position. 'It is about the size of Ashted without the three gentlemen's houses in it . . . . A village much in decay; in the streets are immense masses of stones and holes, and dung all about, houses like a farm kitchen, with this difference that there are the stables underneath.' It was not even large enough to hold the whole staff, but it was near the front, it was in the middle of good fox-hunting country and, best of all, it was well away from the intrigues of Cadiz and Lisbon.

In the six months which he spent at Freineda Wellington laid the plans for his next offensive. The first moves were unobtrusive. In February he asked for a siege-train to be sent to Coruña. At the same port, also, was built up through the spring a fleet of transports loaded with ammunition and food. These were ostensibly for the benefit of the Spanish Army of Galicia but seldom actually unloaded any of their cargoes.

It was clear that for the opening of the campaign the Allies would for the first time have a numerical superiority. With the infantry of the Army of

Portugal detached to assist Clausel in the north Joseph and Jourdan had only about 60,000 of all arms on their wide front. Against them Wellington could bring more than 100,000 men with 102 guns. Eighty-one thousand of these troops made up the Anglo-Portuguese army and the remaining 21,000 represented the Spanish Fourth Army, the only Spanish troops which could be got to the front in time. While the King could hope in time for the support of the six divisions of the Army of Portugal and of two divisions of the Army of the North, he could count on no help from Marshal Suchet on the east coast. The long-delayed expedition from Sicily had at last arrived and despite having changed commanders four times in as many months had succeeded in defeating Suchet in a somewhat unconvincing manner at Castalla near Alicante in April. On Wellington's instructions it was now re-embarking with as many Spanish troops as could be gathered together and was due to arrive before Tarragona in May where its appearance could be counted upon to keep the Armies of Aragon and Valencia firmly tied to their own territory.

Wellington had hoped to move forward in the first week in May, but the crops were late and without green forage the horses would starve on the advance. Moreover the cumbersome bridging-train which was vital to his plan moved with excruciating slowness and was not in position for weeks after it was due. It was not until the third week in May that the French command were relieved of their anxiety about a thrust up the valley of the Tagus, when Hill's corps started to move northward from Alcantara towards the pass of Perales and Ciudad Rodrigo. A French cavalry reconnaissance at the same time found no signs of activity on the north bank of the Douro. It was now becoming clear to them that the main thrust was to come, as in 1812, up the Salamanca road. Around Rodrigo Wellington was showing himself for all to see, at a series of reviews. For a short time the fears of the French command were allayed. They could pursue their plan of checking the Allies behind the Douro and gain time for the concentration of their whole force.

On 22nd May the advance began. As he crossed the frontier Wellington 'turned round his horse, took off his hat, and said "Farewell Portugal! I shall never see you again".'[*] As his advance-guard there rode six brigades of cavalry, an impenetrable screen. They were followed by the Light Division, who had always led the army's advances. Behind this imposing

---

[*] This story comes from a letter to William Napier from Sir R. Donkin who heard the anecdote from Picton. Donkin adds: 'This was so theatrical – so unlike Wellington – that I should say at once it cannot be true; but Picton who told it me was truth itself'. It seems improbable that Picton was present at the time as the Third Division was many miles away.

front there was little; only Hill's corps, the Second Division and the Portuguese Division, strengthened by two small Spanish divisions. On the fourth day the cavalry reached the outskirts of Salamanca and almost cut off the garrison which was slow in getting away.

King Joseph immediately gave orders for the concentration of his whole force between Toro and Tordesillas. By the end of the month at least 50,000 men should be available in that strong position behind a broad river and if Wellington could be checked there as many men again could be added to the King's strength. The royal headquarters, if somewhat nervous, were confident that the situation was in hand.

Then doubts began to intervene. Wellington halted at Salamanca and rumours came through that something was afoot on the north bank of the Douro. The full purport of these last was confirmed on 2nd June when the 10th Hussars charged in on two regiments of French cavalry at Morales, six miles east of Toro on the flank of the Douro position, and drove them in disorder on to the French infantry. One French regiment was almost destroyed.

At last Joseph and Jourdan realised what was happening. Thomas Graham, with 42,000 infantry and cavalry, the First, Third, Fourth, Fifth, Sixth and Seventh Divisions had crossed the Douro inside the Portuguese frontier and had concentrated around Bragança. While the French attention had been drawn to Salamanca they had crossed the mountains of Tras os Montes by tracks which the French had counted impassable and emerged, undetected, on to the plains of Leon. At the crossing of the Esla, a hazardous business, since the river was high, the advance-guard of the infantry had to swim across holding to the stirrups and tails of the cavalry horses, a French cavalry piquet was captured entire before being able to give the alarm. The position on the Douro was turned in overwhelming strength before it was even partially manned. By 4th June the whole of the Anglo-Portuguese army was on the north bank of the Douro in a compact mass of 80,000 men. On the south bank there was only a Spanish division which had been left as a garrison for Salamanca. Less than 20 miles to the north the Spanish Army of Galicia was ready to move eastward on a parallel line and if its commander's belated report that there was no reserve of ammunition infuriated Wellington this fact was not known to the enemy.

Joseph determined to retreat and to retreat far and fast. Although he put the bulk of his infantry into a delaying position on the Pisuerga river he had no intention of standing there and pushed on to Burgos. This was as well since the bulk of the Allied army was flooding round his northern flank in three great columns while only negligible numbers followed the line of his retreat.

On 10th June the whole Allied army was crossing the Pisuerga west and north-west of Burgos with no sign of a Frenchman to their front. That day Wellington set in train the second part of his scheme. He wrote to the senior British officer at Coruña 'There are in Coruña certain ships loaded with biscuit and flour, and certain others loaded with a heavy train of artillery and ammunition, and some musket ammunition, and I shall be very much obliged if you will request any officer of the navy who may be at Coruña when you receive this letter to take under his convoy all the vessels loaded as mentioned above, and to proceed with them to Santander. If he should find Santander occupied by the enemy, I beg him to remain off the port till the operations of this army have obliged the enemy to abandon it.'

The stake was now nothing less than the liberation of the whole French kingdom of Spain. Lisbon, which had been the British base since 1808 was to be abandoned and the lines of communication changed from the long overland haul from the mouth of the Tagus to the short but mountainous roads from the Biscay coast. At a time when he was forcing the French drastically to shorten their communications with France, Wellington, by an imaginative use of sea-power, saved several weeks from the time that men and supplies took in reaching the army from England.

The French formed up to cover Burgos. Joseph by this time had eight and a half divisions in hand and another was close behind, but again the Allies were past their northern wing. There was nothing for it but another retreat, this time to the line of the Ebro. Early on the morning of 13th June a vast explosion announced to the troops of Wellington's most southerly column that the French had destroyed the castle of Burgos, the fortification that had proved such a stumbling-block to the campaign of the previous year.

On the line of the Ebro, astride the main road to France, Joseph disposed the 60,000 men who now comprised his army between Frias and Haro. No enemy was to his front. Wellington had again swung northward. For three days the Allies marched over inhospitable foothills of the Cantabrian mountains 'over the most monotonous and uninteresting country I ever beheld – without wood, feature, verdure, streams of water, picturesque villages or any one recommendation. Scarcely anything could be purchased to help out the homely fare of ship-biscuit, rum and lean ration beef, which was alive and merry in the morning, and consumed before night.'

By the 16th all the Allied columns were across the Ebro at Rocamunde and Puente Arenas, and the Galicians were pressing forward for a demonstration to the gates of Bilbao. The valley of the Ebro was a revelation to the troops after their years of campaigning in the uplands of

Portugal and the cornlands of Leon. 'What was our excessive delight on suddenly and unexpectedly beholding an extensive valley at our feet through which flowed the rapid Ebro; and that valley as well as the country for miles beyond, teaming with fresh woods, fruit trees, beautiful villages and everything which could delight the eye.'

The French had lost track of the Allies; they had seen nothing more than Spanish cavalry since 12th June, and it was not until the 17th that they realised that the line of the Ebro was turned. They had no option but to retreat at their best speed. Even so they miscalculated, believing that Wellington intended to drive on Bilbao while, in fact, he was heading straight to Vitoria, hoping to cut the main road to France in their rear. Reille with the three divisions of the Army of Portugal was ordered to march north to join with Foy who was known to be somewhere in that direction.

In attempting to carry out these orders Reille brought on the first fighting since 2nd June. With two of his divisions he all but ran headlong into three British divisions at Osma. Seeing himself outnumbered Reille turned about, and marched back to the main army, having lost about a hundred men. His other division, Maucune's, had a more lively day. Having held the extreme right of the French position on the Ebro at Frias, Maucune was retreating to join his chief by a short cut through the hills. He was surprised by the Light Division at San Milan and his division was so roughly handled that three days later King Joseph preferred to use it as a baggage-guard rather than let it help toward swelling his inadequate numbers at the Battle of Vitoria.

Next day, 19th June, the French army began to stream into the Plain of Vitoria. Two of Wellington's three columns were close behind him. The third, Graham's, now headed by a division of Cantabrian light infantry, 3,500 strong under the guerrilla leader Longa, was moving towards the northern side of the plain making for the road that led from Vitoria to Bilbao. The rest of the army had, on 20th June, the first day of rest that it had enjoyed since crossing the Portuguese frontier a month before. In that time they had advanced 250 miles as the crow flies from Ciudad Rodrigo, driving the enemy before them without engaging in anything more serious than four skirmishes. It was an astonishing achievement. Not only was the tactical conception far beyond anything that the French had believed possible, but the logistic achievement was perhaps the most remarkable in military history. For a month 100,000 men with their thousands of horses and mules had been constantly provided with everything it needed by means of a vast train of bullock carts and mules employed over ever-lengthening distances. At no time was any unit seriously short of rations. 'I never saw the army in such order', wrote a cavalry officer, at half distance, 'and the sick have decreased.'

One of the Anglo-Portuguese divisions, the Sixth, was not brought forward to Victoria but was halted at Medina de Pomar with orders 'to cover the march of our magazines and stores'. Wellington has been criticised for denying himself the use of this major formation in the battle that was fought on the 21st, but although it was never engaged it might have played a very vital part in the campaign. There were, within a few days' march of Vitoria, two bodies of French troops which together numbered some 20,000 men. Foy with a quarter of this number was known to be in the area of Bilbao. Clausel with the remainder was somewhere in Navarre. Neither Wellington nor King Joseph had any definite information of their whereabouts and it would have been criminal folly on Wellington's part if he had left his rear and his lines of communication open to attack by such large and unlocated bodies of the enemy. Clausel was, in fact, at the crucial time marching up the valley of the Ebro in obedience to an out-of-date order from the King to join him at Miranda and might well have struck in at Wellington's rear had circumstances over which the Allied commander had no control not made him swerve aside.

Joseph's decision to stand at Vitoria was a compound of hope and despair. He hoped that Wellington would continue the policy of turning his right flank which he had steadfastly pursued since the Douro. Thus he hoped that the main body of the Allies would move on Bilbao and the coastal plains rather than attempt to drive the French through the narrow defiles of the mountains of Cantabria. If Wellington did this, Joseph believed that Clausel and Foy would have time to join him and that together they would have sufficient strength to take the offensive against the Allied rear. Despair played an equal part. The troops were losing heart daily. They had been retreating continuously for a month in the face of an enemy which few of them had ever seen. Every day faith in the high command grew weaker and tactical withdrawals seemed more and more like running away. Worse still was the King's fear of the terrible wrath of his brother if he evacuated his kingdom and laid France open to invasion without making at least one attempt to save it by a defensive battle. Finally, there was in Vitoria a vast collection of refugees, Spaniards who had embraced his cause and French civilian officials, a vast collection of paintings and other valuables, including 5,000,000 francs in gold which had just arrived from France as a contribution towards the long-overdue pay of the army. Such a train could not move at the speed of the field army and time must be made to give it a reasonable start on its way to France. Convoys bearing the first instalments of this impedimenta were sent off on 20th and 21st June under escort of Maucune's division but much, including all the gold, never left Vitoria.

In this mood, Joseph set about taking up the strongest position he could find in the Plain of Vitoria. He had available eight and a half infantry divisions, some 9,000 horse and 104 guns, apart from a large arsenal of cannon belonging to the Army of the North which was stored in the city. In all the French army totalled about 57,000 men exclusive of non-combatants. But Joseph's chief hope lay in the arrival of Clausel who, he was convinced would join him with his 15,000 men 'on the 21st at the latest'.

Against him Wellington was bringing an Allied army of about 75,000 of whom rather more than 7,000 were Spanish. The force included 8,000 cavalry and 75 guns.

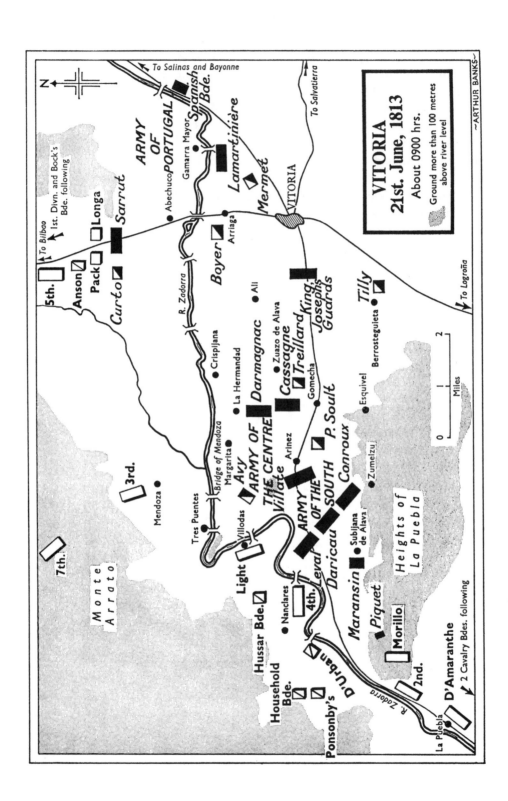

VITORIA
21st. June, 1813
About 0900 hrs.

Ground more than 100 metres
above river level

~ARTHUR BANKS~

9

Vitoria – 21st June 1813

The city of Vitoria lies towards the eastern end of an oval of rolling ground which measures about 12 miles from east to west and about seven miles from north to south. The River Zadorra flows into the north-eastern side of the oval through the defile of Salinas and out through another defile north of the village of La Puebla. The river is fast-flowing but fordable in many places, although high banks make fording difficult. Across the oval the river meanders. Past the city the general direction is westerly until it reaches, near the village of Tres Puentes, an isolated hillock round three sides of which it winds tightly before taking a generally southerly direction. The great road to Bayonne runs alongside the river through both the defiles, but across the oval it cuts straight across the open country passing through the city. Vitoria is the junction of many roads, of which the more important are those which run north-west to Bilbao, south to Trevino and the Ebro valley and east to Pamplona.

On the day before the battle, Jourdan was kept in his bed by a fever and the disposition of the troops fell to Joseph, who, though well-meaning, had few military qualifications. Insofar as he expected to be attacked at all, Joseph seems to have believed that the principal danger was of an attack up the main road through the defile of La Puebla. To guard against this he ordered the largest of his three armies, that of the South, four and a half divisions under Count Gazan, to take up a position astride the main road with his centre in front of Arinez, his right near the Zadorra, in the direction of Villodas, and his left on the hills which separate the Madrid and Trevino roads. Three divisions held this line while the fourth, Villatte's was in reserve near Arinez. The independent brigade of Maransin held the village of Subijana de Alava as an advance post. Ample artillery was available, Gazan having 54 guns under his command. Joseph and Gazan would have wished to include the Puebla defile in the position, but both felt that to do so would overstretch the army's resources, and they contented themselves with posting a strong piquet of *voltigeurs* on the steep crest above the road.

The second line was held by the two divisions of the Army of the Centre under Count d'Erlon. All the infantry were drawn up between the villages of Margarita and Gomecha. Part of d'Erlon's responsibility was to guard the crossings of the Zadorra in the immediate rear of the Army of the South, especially the bridges of Villodas, Tres Puentes and Mendoza. To this task he allocated no more than two regiments of cavalry; fewer than 500 men.

General Reille, with the two available divisions of the Army of Portugal, was originally ordered to form a third line in front of Vitoria itself, but the fear that the Allies might once more have swung northward caused the King to re-post them north of the city, watching the Bilbao road. They thus took up a position with their backs to the Army of the South and with some five miles between the main positions of the two armies. On their right, 2,000 of the King's Spanish troops, men of doubtful loyalty, stiffened by about a thousand men from detachments of the Army of the North collected during the retreat, watched the river crossings near the Salinas defile. A cavalry reconnaissance up the Bilbao road had met some Spanish troops which were believed to be creating a diversion from the real point of danger, but fears about an attack from this direction were aroused on the night of 20th/21st June when a deserter came into Gazan's lines with a report that Wellington with a large body of troops had marched off northward at dusk.

Wellington intended to inflict a decisive defeat on the French by cutting them off from the main road to France. He divided his army into four columns. On the right Rowland Hill with 30,000 men was to secure the defile of La Puebla and drive up the main road towards Vitoria. The troops under his command were of the Second Division and the Portuguese division, now headed by the Portuguese general, the Conde d'Amaranthe. To these were added a Spanish division commanded by Morillo and two cavalry brigades. These were the only troops that did not have an opposed river crossing in prospect as they were to ford the Zadorra well outside the French position. On the extreme left Thomas Graham with a column of similar strength, which had moved north to Murguia on 20th June, was to strike in behind Vitoria by the Bilbao road, and 'if. . . he observes that the troops forming the right of the army continue to advance, he will . . . turn his whole attention to cutting off the retreat of the enemy by the great road which goes from Vitoria by Tolosa and Irun to France'. For this task he was allotted the First and Fifth Divisions, two independent Portuguese brigades, Longa's five battalions of Cantabrian light infantry and two cavalry brigades.

The Third and Seventh Divisions, forming the left centre column under the Earl of Dalhousie, who were around Zuazo on the night of 20th June, were to cross the rugged Monte Arato and cross the the Zadorra by and near the bridge of Mendoza, to the east of the Tres Puentes 'appendix'. Wellington himself retained command of the right centre column, made up of the Fourth and Light Divisions with the remaining four brigades of cavalry and intended to put it across the river by the bridges of Nanclares and Villodas, on the right flank of the Army of the South. Dalhousie's column was rather more than 14,000 strong and Wellington's numbered 13,000 infantry and 4,500 cavalry.

Early on the morning of 21st June Marshal Jourdan, recovered from his fever, rode out with King Joseph to inspect the positions of the French army. They had no sense of urgency in their ride. 'No information', wrote Jourdan, 'had reached us which suggested an immediate attack'. Both of them were troubled by the wide dispersion of the army, by the five miles that lay between the Army of the South and the Army of Portugal. This so struck them that they agreed that the Army of the South would be better disposed on the spur Gomecha-La Hermandad. They had already sent to Gazan asking him to ride over to discuss this alteration when a message from him reached them saying that heavy columns were advancing against his front on the east bank of the river. It was now too late to think of changing position and the commanders rode forward to the right flank of Gazan's army, where Leval's division held a prominent mound to the south of Villodas.

Hill's attack up the line of the main road did not develop very fast. His first care was to send a brigade of Morillo's Spaniards up the steep hillside to his right to secure the defile. 'The ascent', wrote an observer from the other side of the river, 'was so steep that, while moving up it, they looked as if they were lying on their faces or crawling'. With their second brigade in support the Spaniards drove away the *voltigeurs* and established themselves on the crest, but Gazan, realising the danger hurried up the nearest troops available, Maransin's brigade which formed his advance-guard. Hill, therefore, ordered Cadogan's brigade to turn off to their right to support Morillo. Cadogan led up the slope at the head of his own battalion, the 71st Highlanders, covered by the light companies of the brigade, while behind him there was some confusion of order and counter-order. 'The 50th and 92nd regiments were ordered to support the attack on the heights. These troops had nearly gained the summit when they received an order to return. We had descended about half way when a third order arrived, for the 50th regiment to proceed to their first destination, and the 92nd to attack a French battalion of infantry, posted on a ridge a little in their front.' Meanwhile as the 71st approached the crest the French 'opened a tremendous fire from the rocks above and killed a great number. The noble colonel still urging his men forward, we had to make our way through trees and undergrowth. The French now began to retreat from rock to rock, still keeping a destructive fire on us, our men falling right and left. Our Colonel (who was mounted on a favourite chestnut English charger) whose eye was everywhere, perceived a French column trying to outflank Captain Hall's company, and turning round on his horse to give orders for another company to reinforce them, received a ball in the back from a French *chasseur*.' The 71st reached the crest and halted to reform, but Cadogan was dying. He asked for his head to be propped up on a haversack and 'wished to be brought nearer to the edge of the precipice that he might have a better view of the line. He asked where was Lord Wellington and I [his quarter-master] pointed him out surrounded by his staff. The wind from the plain was piercingly cold, and I begged him to allow me to remove him, but he said, "Let me remain, I trust in God that this will be a glorious day for England".'

Gazan's decision to counter-attack on the heights with Maransin's brigade was ill-conceived. By doing so he laid open the front of his main position and O'Callaghan's brigade occupied Subijana de Alava without significant resistance. 'The enemy opened on us with fourteen pieces of artillery, from their position, as we moved down, but with little effect. I could never persuade myself that they would resign so important a post as the village without a struggle; and when we got close to it, and began to find the ground difficult and intersected with walls and banks, I expected every moment to be saluted with a murderous discharge of musquetry, and to see them issue forth. Not a soul, however, was in the village; but a wood a few hundred yards to the left, and the ravines above it, were filled with French light troops.' The light companies were directed to advance and clear the wood. 'A field of corn standing four or five feet high, and just ready for the sickle, was between us and the wood, and as we advanced through it, beside the bullets from the wood, an occasional cannon ball bowled along through it, its course being easily seen by the lowering of the ears of corn as if reaped. As we approached the wood, the fire from it slackened, and we entered and passed through without meeting much opposition; but when we emerged at the opposite side, we saw the dark line of the French army, still in their position, within point-blank range.' Here the attack halted, not because either the commanders or the troops believed the French line unassailable, but on orders from Wellington, who was becoming increasingly concerned at the failure to appear of his left and the left centre columns.

The French were also facing problems. Gazan could see, on the west bank of the river a great mass of British and Portuguese troops halted around the village of Nanclares. These were the Fourth and Light Divisions with the Hussar brigade in close support waiting for Wellington to give the word for them to assault the bridges. 'This tranquility on the part of the enemy on my right', wrote Gazan, 'gave me the idea that the enemy attack on my left [Hill's] was not the real thrust and that it was only made in order to make us weaken our right by moving our forces to meet it. I suggested this to the King, but the idea was hardly considered. Marshal Jourdan announcing loudly and publicly that all the movements on our right were feints to which no attention must be paid, and that if we lost the battle it would be because the mountains on the left of the Zadorra remained in enemy hands.' Gazan was therefore ordered to detach his only reserve division, Villatte's, from its position near Arinez to march through Zumelzu to the crest of the Puebla heights from whence it was to attack along the high ground and drive the British and the Spaniards down into the defile from which they had climbed. Gazan's centre and left-hand divisions, those of Conroux and Daricau, were to support this drive by counter-attacking at Subijana. Following his obsession with an attack from the south Jourdan ordered a division of dragoons to Berrosteguieta to block the Trevino road and sent an infantry division from the Army of the Centre to support them.

Although Wellington still saw no sign of the arrival of Graham or Dalhousie, he now received a piece of most opportune information. He was on the point of ordering the Light Division to storm the bridge of Villodas which appeared to be strongly held, when a peasant came up to him with the news that the bridge of Tres Puentes was unguarded. Instantly modifying his plan, Wellington ordered Kempt's brigade of the Light Division to follow the peasant. Almost simultaneously an outbreak of firing to the north-east announced that Graham was in action on the Bilbao road and the leading scarlet columns of Dalhousie's corps were seen on the slopes of Monte Arato.

Kempt's brigade 'moved off by threes at a rapid pace along a very uneven and circuitous path (which was concealed from the observation of the French by high rocks), and reached the narrow bridge. The 1st Rifles led the way, and the whole brigade following, passed at a run, with firelocks and rifles ready cocked, and ascended a steep road of fifty yards, at the top of which was an old chapel. We had no sooner cleared it than we observed a heavy column of the French on the principal hill, and commanding a bird's eye view of us . . . . The regiments formed at top speed, without any word of command. Two round shots now came amongst us: the second severed the head from the body of our bold guide, the Spanish peasant . . . . Sir James Kempt expressed much surprise at our critical position, and our not being molested, and sent his aide-de-camp at speed across the river for the 15th Hussars, who came forward singly and at a gallop up the steep path and dismounted behind our centre. Some French dragoons coolly and at a slow pace, came up to within fifty yards of us, to examine if possible our strength, but a few shots from the Rifles caused them to decamp.'

Kempt had arrived behind the flank of the Army of the South, in the stretch of river for which responsibility had been allocated to two cavalry regiments of the Army of the Centre, a force quite inadequate to resist the attack of an infantry brigade. Nor could the French easily send infantry support. The Army of the Centre had already detached one of its divisions towards the Trevino road and the other was increasingly preoccupied with the deployment of Dalhousie's column around Mendoza. The Army of the South was in no better position to help. At this moment Villatte was developing his attack along the Puebla heights and two more divisions were largely committed to supporting it, leaving only Leval's division intact upon the main position.

Up on the heights, Villatte won a temporary success. The major to whom command of the 71st had fallen on Cadogan's death unwisely ordered the battalion to advance against the new and powerful French force. 'Immediately we charged up the hill, the piper playing "Hey Johnny Cope". The French had possession of the top but we soon forced them back, and drew up in column on the height; sending out four companies to our left to skirmish. The remainder moved on to the opposite height. As we advanced, driving them before us, a French officer, a pretty fellow, was pricking and forcing his men to stand. They heeded him not.

'Scarce were we upon the height, when a heavy column, dressed in great coats with white covers on their hats, exactly resembling the Spanish, gave us a volley, which put us to the right about in double quick time down the hill, the French close behind through the whins. The four companies got the word, the French were on them. They likewise thought them Spaniards, until they got a volley, that killed or wounded almost every one of them. We retired to the heights covered by the 50th, who gave them a volley which checked their speed. We moved up the remains of our shattered regiment to the height. Being in great want of ammunition, we were again served with sixty rounds a man, and kept up our fire.'

The French pressed on and at one stage had reached to within a few yards of the western height when the timely arrival of the 92nd Highlanders halted their advance. Twice they renewed their advance but each time they were repulsed and by then events in the plain made the fighting on the Puebla heights irrelevant. Nor was the counter-attack in the plains any more successful. O'Callaghan's brigade, though hard pressed, managed to maintain their position in Subijana.

Around Mendoza the head of Dalhousie's column stood waiting. With them was Sir Thomas Picton, who was very angry. When, on the previous evening, Captain Staveley of the Royal Staff Corps had handed him his orders he had exclaimed, "D− the Quartermaster-General".★ 'There-upon', wrote Stavely, 'I took off my cocked hat and asked him if he had any orders for me. He, also, taking off his hat and making a low bow, replied, "None, Sir".' Sir Thomas was angry because his division had been put under the command of Dalhousie, an officer for whose capabilities Picton had but slight regard but who happened to be his senior in the Army List. Now, as he waited at Mendoza, he was angry because although the Third Division was ready and waiting to go, only one brigade of the Seventh Division had arrived and Lord Dalhousie was not with it. As one of his staff wrote: 'General Picton was impatient; he enquired of several aides-de-camp who came near him from head-quarters, whether they had any orders for him? As the day wore on, and the fight waxed warmer on the right, he became furious, and observed, "D− it! Lord Wellington must have forgotten us!" Picton's blood was boiling, and his stick was going with rapid strokes upon the mane of his cob; he was riding backwards and forwards, looking in every direction for the arrival of an aide-de-camp, until at length one galloped up from Lord Wellington, suddenly checked his horse and demanded of the general whether he had seen Lord Dalhousie. Picton was disappointed; he expected now at least that he might move; and, in a voice which did not gain softness from his feelings, he answered in a sharp tone, "No, sir! I have not seen his lordship; but have you any orders for me, sir?" . . . "None", replied the aide-de-camp . . . . "Then pray, sir", continued the irritated general, "what are the orders that you *do* bring?" . . . "Why", answered the officer, "that as soon as Lord Dalhousie, with the seventh division, shall commence an attack upon the bridge, the fourth and light divisions are to support him." Picton, drawing himself up to his full height, said to the astonished aide-de-camp with some passion, "You may tell Lord Wellington from me, sir, that the third division under my command shall in less than ten minutes attack the bridge and carry it, and the fourth and light divisions may support if they choose." Having thus expressed his intention, he turned from the aide-de-camp and put himself at the head of his soldiers, encouraging them with the bland appellation of "Come on, ye rascals! Come on, ye fighting villains!" '

The advance of the Third Division was a great relief to the men of Kempt's brigade in their advanced position 'in the elbow of the French position, and isolated from the rest of the army, within a hundred yards of the enemy and absolutely occupying part of his position'. A Rifleman

---

★ In Wellington's army the Quartermaster-General performed the functions which today would be carried out by the 'G' staff.

recalled how they 'observed from our left the bayonets of the third division glittering above the standing corn, and advancing upon another bridge which stood about a quarter of a mile to our left, and where on their arrival they were warmly opposed by the enemy's light troops, who lined the bank of the river, (which we ourselves were now on) in great force, for the defence of the bridge. As soon as this was observed, Colonel Barnard advanced with our battalion [1st Rifles] and took them in flank with such a furious fire as quickly dislodged them, and thereby opened a passage free of expense, which must other wise have cost them dearly. What with the rapidity of our movement, the colour of our dress, and the close contact with the enemy, we had the misfortune to be identified with them for some time, by a battery of our own guns, who not observing our movement, continued to serve it out indiscriminately, and all the while admiring their practice upon us; nor was it until the red coats of the third division joined us, that they discovered their mistake.'

Away to the north-east, Graham found one division of the Army of Portugal drawn up on a spur in front of the village of Abechuco, supported by cavalry, while Reille's other division lined the bank of the Zadorra, a mile to the rear. Against the forward division, Graham deployed Longa's Cantabrians and Pack's Portuguese brigade. The French did not make a very convincing stand in this position and the *caçadores* of Pack's brigade drove them from the heights with the bayonet. From this point Graham moved forward cautiously. He had been ordered to regulate his movements by the progress on his right and Dalhousie's dilatoriness delayed Graham as it did Picton. Nevertheless he sent Longa against the bridge of Durana and by noon the high road to Bayonne was effectively blocked by fire although it was not until the early afternoon that the Cantabrians succeeded in forcing a crossing in the face of a stubborn defence by their renegade compatriots, who unlike Longa's men were supported by artillery. Downstream the Fifth Division was directed against the village of Gamarra Mayor, which the French were holding as a bridge-head. The leading brigade, Robinson's, did not make a convincing attack and was brought to a halt. 'There was some shyness in the two leading regiments, or some misunderstanding of orders; but Colonel Brooke perceiving it called out, "Come on, Grenadiers 4th!", passed the other two with his battalion, and carried the place, taking two thousand prisoners and three guns.' Further advance was impossible. The Fifth Division made a series of attempts to force a way across the bridge but all were beaten back with heavy loss, and it was not until five o'clock that a firm footing was gained on the far bank. Graham did not see fit to commit the First Division and without them the forces engaged were too evenly matched for a decisive result to be achieved.

By this time even Marshal Jourdan was convinced that the main Allied threat was not to his left flank. He and the King therefore decided to retreat to a line in front of Vitoria. Gazan remonstrated strongly that two-thirds of the Army of the South were closely engaged and that to disengage them would be more dangerous than to stand and fight it out on their present position. He was ordered to fall back by stages to a position which Jourdan would point out to him. This was the last order that he received that day and, being a literal-minded officer, he retired his army, brigade by brigade, and took up nothing more than a series of delaying positions for the rest of the day, his infantry playing no part in the attempt to stand outside Vitoria.

While Gazan was beginning his disengagement, Picton advanced on Arinez, the key to the Army of the South's position. Brisbane's brigade was directed to take it and went forward behind a screen composed of the two companies of the 95th Rifles. Wellington rode amongst the Riflemen calling out, "That's right, my lads! Keep up a good fire", while at the head of the Third Division, 'old Picton rode . . . dressed in a blue coat and a round hat, and swore as roundly as if he had been wearing two cocked ones'. The Rifles tore into Arinez, but were checked and 'at one period, we held one side of a wall, while the French were on the other side, so that any person who chose to put his head over from either side was sure of getting a sword or a bayonet up his nostrils'. The French stand was not of long duration, for Brisbane's brigade in line swept through and passed the village driving the French before them.

Meanwhile Lord Dalhousie was forming his only available brigade on Picton's left and the Fourth Division had surged over the bridge of Villodas, left uncovered by Picton's advance. The second brigade of the Light Division, Vandeleur's, was ordered across, behind Picton's rear to support Dalhousie, and Vandeleur sent his Brigade Major, Captain Harry Smith, to the Seventh Division, then held up in front of La Hermandad, for orders. 'I found his lordship and his Q.M.G., Drake, an old Rifle comrade, in deep conversation. I reported pretty quick, and asked for orders (the head of my Brigade was just getting under fire). I repeated the question "What orders, my Lord?" Drake became somewhat animated, and I heard His Lordship say, "Better take the village", which the French held with twelve guns (I had counted their fire) and seemed inclined to keep it. I roared out, "Certainly, my Lord", and off I galloped, both calling to me to come back, but as none are so deaf as those who won't hear, I told General Vandeleur we were immediately to take the village. There was no time to lose, and the 52nd Regiment deployed into line as if at Shorncliffe, while our Riflemen were sent out in all directions, five or six deep, keeping up the firing that nothing could resist. I galloped to the officer in command of a Battalion of the 7th Division (the 82nd, I think). "Lord Dalhousie desires you closely to follow this brigade of the Light Division." "Who are you, sir?" "Never mind that; disobey my Lord's order at your peril." My Brigade, the 52nd in line and the swarms of Riflemen, rushed at the village, and although the ground was intersected in its front by gardens and ditches, nothing ever checked us until we reached the rear of the village, where we halted to reform . . . the twelve guns, tumbrils, horses, etc., standing in our possession. There never was a more impetuous onset . . . nothing could withstand such a burst of determination. Before we were ready to pursue the enemy . . . for we Light Division ever reformed and got into order before a second attack, thanks to poor General Bob Craufurd's most excellent tuition . . . up came Lord Dalhousie to old Vandeleur, exclaiming, "Most brilliantly achieved indeed! Where is the officer you sent to me for orders?" "Here I am, my Lord." "Upon my word, sir, you receive and carry orders quicker than any officer I ever saw." "You said, 'Take the village.' My Lord, there it is!" I said, "guns and all".'

With La Hermandad lost, the French were back on to their final position. This was on the line Crispijana-Zuazo de Alva-Gomecha-Esquival, with the northern end allocated to the Army of the Centre and the southern to the Army of the South, but although the latter's artillery unlimbered on the position and opened a heavy fire, the infantry made no serious stand. Gazan received no indication of where he was to form and continued his retreat. Behind the line orders were given to get away the vast acccumulation of stores, artillery, treasure and hangers-on which still encumbered the streets and surroundings of Vitoria. Since Longa had cut the main road to Bayonne, there was no way out for this mass of vehicles except the rough and narrow country road that led eastward to Pamplona by way of Salvatierra. It was not long before this line of escape was jammed and impassable to vehicles.

In front of the French position, Wellington paused while the allied artillery was brought to the front. For a time the battle developed into an artillery duel with some 75 guns on each side battering each other. Only at Gamarra Mayor, where the Fifth Division continued unsuccessfully to try to force the bridge, did the infantry fight continue.

At last Wellington gave the word, and the long British line went forward. Near the river marched the Seventh Division. On their right, in succession, the Third, Fourth and Second, while Morillo's Spaniards and their British supports swung in on the French flank from the eastern end of the Puebla heights. Only near the river was there appreciable infantry resistance and this quickly disintegrated when the Hussar brigade cut in between the right of the ever-retreating Army of the South and the left of the steadfast Army of the Centre. The appearance of the hussars in and around Vitoria, where the baggage and artillery were already inextricably mixed, turned chaos into panic. The drivers cut their traces and made off astride the draught horses, leaving the wagons and carriages immobile in the narrow road. The retreating infantry of the Army of the South, seeing the road blocked in front of them, broke their ranks and took to the by-ways or joined the ever-growing number of camp-followers, Spanish peasants and British hussars who set to looting the vast store of coin and valuables that crowded the roads.

Seeing his retreat threatened, Reille ordered the Army of Portugal back from the line of the Zadorra, and the Fifth Division was at last able to go forward over the bridge of Gamarra Mayor with Graham's two cavalry brigades taking the lead. Of the three French armies only that of Portugal went back in something approaching good order. Reille with Fririon's brigade flanked by his cavalry covered the rear of the whole army into the valley that led to Salvatierra. There was little Allied cavalry forward, and that which was available found the ground most unsuitable for mounted action. The leading squadron commander of the 16th Light Dragoons, which had accompanied Graham's column, described how 'the enemy collected in a wood a rear-guard of six squadrons and a regiment of infantry, while others scattered as light troops in all directions. With this force they occupied the plain about half a mile across, surrounded with wood and ending in a defile, thus keeping the head of the lane, along which we alone would get at them. The Spanish infantry [Longa's] got into a field of corn and down the lane, and on firing a few shots the enemy moved off, and we pushed on after them. My squadron was in advance, and on arriving on the plain formed immediately and advanced to the charge. All was confusion, all calling "go on" before the men had time to get to their places. We got half across before I was able to get them into any form, and had we been allowed one minute more in forming, our advance might have been quicker, and made with much more regularity.

'The enemy had about six squadrons in line, with one a little in advance, consisting of their *élite* companies. This I charged, broke and drove on their line, which, advancing, I was obliged to retire, having had a good deal of sabring with those I charged and with their support. A squadron of the 12th was in my rear, and in place of coming up on my flank following me, so that they only added to the confusion of retiring by mixing with my men. Captain Wrexon's squadron of the 16th then came to the charge. We were so mixed that I could not get my men out of his way, and was obliged to front and make a rally back, and the enemy, seeing the remainder of the brigade coming up, retired through the defile with their cavalry, leaving a square of grenadiers in its mouth. We came close upon them without perceiving they were there. I rode up within a yard of the enemy's infantry; they had their arms on the port, and were as steady as possible, not a man attempting to fire until we began to retire. They certainly might have reached myself and many others with their bayonets had they been allowed. I never saw men more steady and exact to the word of command. On our going about they fired a running volley, which did considerable execution, and then they made off through the defile.'

In this country further pursuit with cavalry was hopeless and the infantry could go no further. They had been marching since three o'clock in the morning and had covered some 20 miles. One soldier of the Second Division recalled: 'I had fired 108 rounds that day and my shoulder was as black as coal.'

As soon as the divisions went into bivouac that night an orgy of plunder broke out. Not only was there money in abundance but enormous quantities of military stores and food. 'Such plenty now prevailed', wrote an officer of the 82nd, 'that I do not suppose there was a man in the field who had not a good meal that night from the stores of the enemy, which were copiously supplied with every comfort, and now came to us very seasonably; for although every man had not an opportunity of partaking in the plunder, yet there was so great an abundance of every necessity brought into the camp that they were enabled to share the provision with each other. We also got a most seasonable supply of those valuable articles – good shoes, taken from the French magazines. Our men have been constantly on the tramp for many weeks together, without having the time or opportunity to get the old ones mended; indeed several of them had marched for the last few days barefooted. Not getting quite enough to supply all my men, I sent the remainder to exchange theirs with the dead men, many of whom were found with much better shoes than their living comrades had on. We likewise obtained a good supply of salt, an article of great luxury in this part of the country, where it is very dear and scarce; and also tobacco, which could not be obtained previous to this day's victory.'

Late in the evening Captain Staveley was sitting much tired, in the house that served for headquarters in Vitoria. 'Lord Wellington entered the room, and in answer to some remark, as I observed that we had had a glorious day, he replied "Yes, and we have got all their artillery", and going into an inner room, where the dinner was prepared, he said "Tell Murray I shall march the army off myself in the morning." I asked, "At what hour?" "When I get up." '

The victory at Vitoria irrevocably broke the French kingdom of Spain. King Joseph narrowly escaped capture at the hands of the Hussar brigade, abandoning his coach and flying on a troop-horse. On hearing of the victory the Russian army sang a *Te Deum*, the only occasion on which this was done for the victory of a foreign army. In Germany, Beethoven composed a 'Battle Symphony' to commemorate the occasion.

The material trophies were enormous:

151	brass ordnance, on travelling carriages
415	caissons
14,249	rounds of ammunition
1,973,400	musket-ball cartridges
40,688	lb. of gunpowder
56	forage waggons
44	forge waggons.

Apart from all this, Captain Freemantle, the aide-de-camp, who carried Wellington's despatch back to England, 'will have the honour of laying at the feet of His Royal Highness the colors of the 4th batt. 100th regiment, and Marshal Jourdan's baton of a Marshal of France taken by the 87th regiment'.

The French army never stopped until it was safely over the border into France. Their last gun was taken from them on 24th June by the 95th Rifles and the Chestnut Troop, so that the sum of their artillery as they re-entered France was one howitzer. Their losses in men had not been enormous, scarcely more than 8,000 but their loss in morale was disastrous. Almost the whole French army, having been overwhelmed in a strong defensive position, had taken to its heels, abandoning not only its heavy equipment but in many cases its personal arms and accoutrements. Few armies have ever been so signally beaten.

The Allied losses were slightly more than 5,000 of whom all but 1,400 were British. The Portuguese suffered 900 casualties and the Spaniards 550. The heaviest losses were in Cadogan's brigade where the 71st lost 350 men and in O'Callaghan's brigade and in the Third Division where two battalions suffered more than 200 casualties. The constant assaults on the bridge of Gamarra Mayor cost the Fifth Division 500 casualties. This was not a heavy loss considering the position that was assailed and carried. Far more serious was the loss of discipline which ensued. 'We started', wrote Wellington, 'with the army in the highest order, and up to the day of the battle nothing could get on better; but that event has, as usual, totally annihilated all order and discipline. The soldiers of the army have got among them about a million in money, which were got for the military chest. The night of the battle, instead of being passed in getting rest and food for the pursuit of the following day, was passed by the soldiers in looking for plunder. The consequence was, that they were incapable of marching in pursuit of the enemy, and were totally knocked up. The rain came on and increased their fatigue, and I am quite convinced that we have now out of the ranks double the number of our loss in the battle; and that we have lost more men in the pursuit than the enemy have; and have never in one day made more than an ordinary march.

'This is the consequence of the state of discipline in the British Army. We may gain the greatest victories; but we shall do no good until we shall so far alter our system, as to force all ranks to perform their duty. The new regiments are, as usual the worst of all. The . . . th Hussars are a disgrace to the name of a soldier, in action as well as elsewhere; and I propose to draft their horses from them, and send the men to England, if I cannot get the better of them in any other manner. I am very apprehensive of the consequence of marching our soldiers through the province of Biscay. It may be depended upon, that the people of this province will shoot them as they would the French, if they should misbehave.'

By the end of June all the French armies were behind their own frontier. Clausel, ignorant of the battle, reached the vicinity of Vitoria on 23rd June to find the place defended by the Sixth Division, which had moved up behind the advance of the main army. He retreated headlong and although Wellington made a spirited attempt to entrap him with five divisions, Clausel managed to regain France with 12,000 men by way of Saragossa and Jaca, leaving 1,500 sick and stragglers on the road. In the north Graham struck at Foy's column but although he managed to engage his rear-guard, he could not prevent the French general from collecting the Biscayan garrisons and marching over the frontier with a force of 16,000 men.

Nevertheless, by the first week of July, the only vestiges of Joseph's kingdom were the fortresses of Pamplona, San Sebastian and Santona, all of them beleaguered and a small strip of land in the Pyrenees, the Val de Baztan, which was relinquished in a few days with no more than a skirmish.*

The mediocre quality of the generalship shown by Joseph and Jourdan should not be allowed to obscure the brilliance of Wellington's Vitoria campaign. The French armies of the North, South, Centre and Portugal mustered between them at least 80,000 men in field formations apart from several thousand more in garrisons. Wellington's advance drove Joseph's

---

* Aragon and Catalonia, which were still occupied by the troops of Marshal Suchet, did not form part of the French kingdom of Spain, having been annexed to France in 1812.

main army straight back on its reinforcements and if it had moved less fast or less skilfully would have enabled the King to concentrate 80,000 first-class French troops at Vitoria or another position of their own choosing so that they could have fought with at least equal numbers against an army with a large proportion of troops whose quality in a set-piece battle was not the equal of French and British units. The basic deficiency of the French command was a lack of appreciation of the ability of their opponent. This error was shared by Napoleon, whose insistence on diverting the infantry of the Army of Portugal to operations in the north made the problem of concentrating the army very much more difficult. To the French, the idea that Wellington could bring 70,000 men from the borders of Portugal to north-eastern Spain was inconceivable. To a French army it would have been impossible. They would have starved, for they had never bothered with organising an efficient supply system, relying for their food on the surrounding countryside, and if there was one thing which the French generals learned it was that in Spain small armies are defeated and large armies starve. Nor could they comprehend Wellington's abandonment of his communications with Lisbon. They had always believed that Wellington was a general who was particularly sensitive about his supply lines. It had not occurred to them that, by calling in the Royal Navy, he could procure a new base with lines of communication as short, if not shorter, than their own.

The Prince Regent summed up the campaign when he wrote, on 3rd July, in his usual exuberant style. 'Your glorious conduct is beyond all human praise, and far above my reward. I know of no language the world affords worthy to express it. I feel I have nothing left to say, but devoutly to offer up my prayer of gratitude to Providence, that it has in its omnipotant bounty, blessed my country and myself with such a General. You have sent me, among the trophies of your unrivalled fame, the staff of a French Marshal, and I send you in return that of England.'

PART FOUR

Wellington and Soult

10

The Passes of the Pyrenees

Napoleon received the first, incomplete, reports of the disaster at Vitoria at Dresden, on 1st July. The campaign on the eastern front had been fought to a standstill and on 4th June he had agreed an armistice with Russia and Prussia. Austria was still the nominal ally of the French, but for some months past she had acted the part of a neutral and the chances of her joining the eastern alliance were increasing daily. The news of the dissolution of the French monarchy in Spain was certain to encourage the alliance to renew the war and Napoleon immediately took steps to save what he could from the wreck. Marshal Soult was sent posting westward to command a unified Army of Spain. He carried with him Napoleon's commission as 'Lieutenant of the Emperor', credits for a million francs, a warrant, for use at his discretion, for the arrest of King Joseph, and instructions 'to re-establish my business in Spain, and to relieve Pamplona and San Sebastian'.

During the eastern armistice a peace conference was held in Prague. Although neither side had any great hopes, or indeed wishes, for the conclusion of a peace, British calculations could not afford to overlook the possibility that some settlement might be reached. In this case the position of the Allied army on the French frontier would become dangerous. 'If', wrote Wellington's Judge Advocate General, 'we are left to Bonaparte's sole attention, we may see Portugal again in spite of the latest glorious victory'. Wellington, therefore, halted on a strong defensive line and waited for further news from Prague.

A pause was also essential on military grounds. The supply situation was very difficult. The change of base from Lisbon to the ports of the Biscayan coast had been carried out, but many loaded transports were held up at Coruña and Lisbon for want of escort, now more than ever needed owing to the activity of American privateers. In this the Royal Navy was at fault. Although their resources were under strain from the American war, enough ships had been allocated to protect the coasts of Spain if only they had not been, in the words of the First Lord of the Admiralty, 'tearing themselves to pieces in long and distant excursions', by which he meant that they were scouring the Atlantic for profitable prizes. Another result of this naval neglect was that the beleaguered

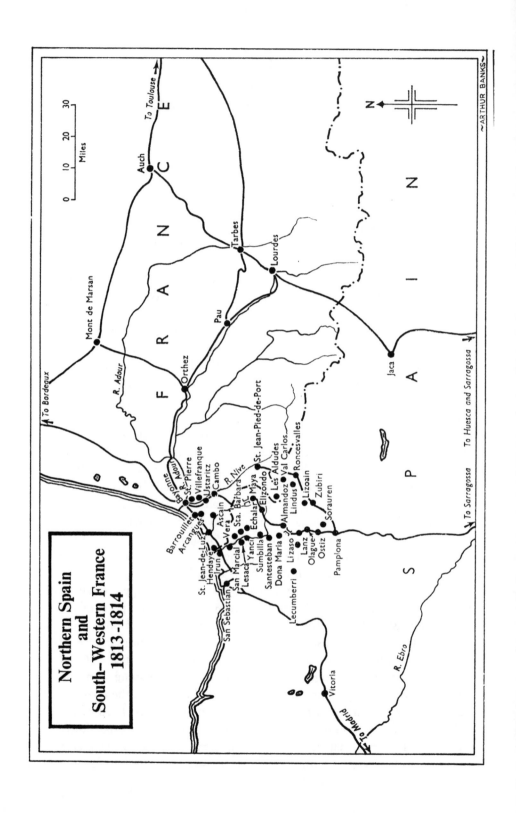

Northern Spain and South-Western France 1813-1814

~ARTHUR BANKS~

French garrison of San Sebastian was able each night to receive supplies and reinforcements by sea.

Above all, Wellington was anxious to rid himself of the fortresses of San Sebastian and Pamplona in his rear, before embarking on the invasion of France. Both were strong and had adequate garrisons, which could cause serious trouble to his lines of communication if the main army was heavily committed beyond the Pyrenees. Since the battering-train was sufficient only for one formal siege, it was devoted to the reduction of San Sebastian and its valuable port, while Pamplona was invested by Spanish troops until starvation should force it to surrender. The rest of the army was stationed in depth along the French frontier to cover the sieges.

At the western end of the front, where the Bidassoa river forms the frontier, Graham commanded a corps composed of the First and Fifth Divisions, a Portuguese brigade and 15,000 Spaniards, which held the river line and besieged San Sebastian. On their right the Seventh and Light Divisions held the pass of Echalar and the heights of Santa Barbara, above Vera. The Val de Baztan was Hill's responsibility, with the Second Division (less one brigade) holding the Maya pass and three Portuguese brigades holding the minor passes to the east as far as Les Aldudes. The right flank of the main army was at the pass of Roncesvalles, where Sir Lowry Cole commanded his own Fourth Division, Byng's brigade from the Second, which held the pass itself, and Morillo's 4,000 Spaniards. This corps, 11,000 strong, was very much larger than anything that Cole had commanded before.

In reserve, were the Sixth Division at Santesteban and the Third at Olague. The cavalry were useless in this mountainous country and, apart from two brigades used for communications behind the front, were quartered around Vitoria. Wellington set up his headquarters at Lesaca, behind the Light Division, at the left centre of the front. It was conceivable that the French might move to their left, unite with Suchet and drive up the valley of the Ebro. Knowing Suchet's disinclination to co-operate with anyone, Wellington discounted this possibility, guarding against it only by posting Mina's guerrilla, now a regular division, around Saragossa to cover his right rear.

Wellington realised that the front was overlong for the number of troops available to guard it. It was always open to the French to concentrate overwhelming strength at one of the possible points of entry, break the tenuous Allied line and debouch into the flatter ground behind. For this purpose they would have the use of a good road system on the north side of the Pyrenees, while the roads on the Spanish side were both poor and unhelpful in direction. Another obstacle to movement on the

Allied side was the Sierra de Aralar, the rugged range that connects the Pyrenees to the mountains of Calabria. The Sierra, crossed by few and inadequate passes, almost isolated the right wing from the centre of the army. Nevertheless Wellington hoped that the forward brigades would be able to defend their positions long enough for the reserve divisions to be concentrated between the beleaguered towns and any French attempt to relieve them.

Soult reached his new army on 12th July and immediately set to work to make a fighting force out of the disorderly and demoralised rabble that had escaped from Vitoria. For this he was extremely well qualified. Born in 1769, the same year as Wellington, he had served in the ranks of the royal army, and rose to be a sergeant before the Revolution. He rose rapidly in rank and reputation in the wars of the Republic. He was especially attached to Masséna, whose chief subordinate he was in the Swiss campaign of 1799 and in the defence of Genoa, where he was wounded and captured. He was one of the original creation of Marshals of the Empire in 1804 and was later created Duke of Dalmatia, a country with which he had no sort of connection. He had borne a prominent part at Austerlitz and arrived in Spain with Napoleon and the *Grande Armée* in 1808. His five-year stay was the longest that any of the marshals achieved, although this may partially have been due to the fact that three years of the time had been spent very comfortably in Andalusia with little to do except to defeat Ballasteros, besiege Cadiz and loot monasteries, all of which he did with great competence. On one of his rare excursions outside his vice-royalty he had been bloodily defeated by Beresford at Albuera. This was not his first defeat at British hands. It was Soult who had pursued Moore to Coruña, where he had raised a handsome monument over his conqueror's grave. Soult was an unsympathetic character, avaricious and disloyal to everyone except the Emperor, but he was an excellent organiser and had a wide and daring strategic sense. His plans for launching his army were usually admirable until he actually got them into battle. Then he faltered. 'Soult', said Wellington, years after Waterloo, 'did not quite understand a field of battle; he knew very well how to bring his troops on to the field, but not so well how to use them when he had brought them up.'

His first actions on reaching Bayonne were a work of genius. Two weeks after his arrival he had reconstituted his army and launched it on an extremely ambitious offensive that all but succeeded in relieving Pamplona. The old and now pathetic titles of the Armies, of the South, the North, the Centre and Portugal were swept away and in their place there was created the Army of Spain. The troops available, after deducting conscripts under training at Bayonne, the three garrisons still holding out in Spain and some 14,000 sick, amounted to 72,000 infantry and 7,000 cavalry, the latter, as with the Allies, of very limited immediate value. The infantry were reorganised into three corps* each of three divisions, and there was in addition a huge Reserve division, 17,000 strong. The arsenal of Bayonne provided an eight-gun battery with each of the ordinary infantry divisions, 32 guns for the Reserve division, two six-gun batteries for the cavalry and a general reserve of 24 guns. To raise the morale of the army, Soult firmly reasserted discipline, while inspiring the troops with a bombastic proclamation blaming their commanders for their recent defeats, urging them to drive the Allies behind the Ebro and ending, 'Let the account of success be dated from Vitoria, and the birthday of the Emperor celebrated from that city.'

Since Suchet refused to co-operate, Soult could choose between three possible lines of advance to relieve one or both of the besieged towns. He could move across the lower Bidassoa, or through the Maya pass or through that of Roncesvalles. Hearing from the governor of San Sebastian that that fortress was in no immediate danger he decided to try first to relieve Pamplona. In this he was encouraged by the isolation of Wellington's right wing and by an underestimate of its strength. To increase the isolation, d'Erlon, with 20,000 men, was to force a way through the Maya pass and seize the passes over the Sierra de Aralar. The two remaining corps were to advance against the Allied right, but, since the narrowness of the Roncesvalles pass precluded the deployment of as much as a single company, only Clausel with his 16,000 men was to make a frontal attack, while Reille, with 15,000, was to advance by a goat-track, four miles to the east of his colleague and separated from him by the deep Val Carlos, aiming for the Lindus plateau on the crest of the Pyrenees. The Bidassoa front was left to the care of the Reserve division. The attack was due to be launched on 24th July but delays forced a postponement for 24 hours and even then few of the French troops had received the rations for four days which had been ordered for them.

Wellington had appreciated Soult's plan wrongly. It was Graham's intention to storm San Sebastian on 24th July and as there was no immediate prospect of the surrender of Pamplona it seemed probable that the French must strike first in the west. Wellington knew that French troops were assembling at the eastern end of the front, but he also knew that bridging-trains were being assembled on the Bidassoa. At midday on 24th July he wrote to Graham on his left wing, 'I have undoubted

---

* Napoleon forbade the establishment of 'corps' but authorised three officers to be nominated as 'lieutenant-generals' with groups of divisions under them.

intelligence that Soult has moved the greatest part of his force towards St. Jean-Pied-de-Port, leaving at Urrugne the boats, which are two complete bridges. It would appear, therefore, that he entertains serious designs to draw our attention from the side of Irun, and then to attempt to pass the river.'

All was ready for the storming on 24th July, but the artillery having set fire to some houses within the breach, the attack, like Soult's, was postponed until the following day.

Wellington was 'very fidgetty' as the time for the storm approached. Writing at midday on the 25th, Larpent described how he 'came out to the churchyard, where we were listening, about eight o'clock, to judge from the noise of the guns whether our batteries had ceased, and what the firing was. He . . . appeared to wish to leave it to Graham, and not directly to interfere. At eleven this morning, however, Colonel Burgh came over with an account of our attempt having failed; that our party (consisting of English, too) went up to the breach, then turned and ran away. Lord Wellington has ordered his horse, and is going over directly.'

While the Commander-in-Chief rode over to San Sebastian to discuss with Graham how best to renew the siege, headquarters at Lesaca heard distant firing from the right. During the afternoon a message came from Lord Dalhousie, at Echalar, saying that a heavy French force had attacked the Pass of Maya and had been repulsed. On the basis of this report General Murray, the Quartermaster-General, sent orders to the commanders of the Seventh and Light Divisions to 'Let your division know that they may have occasion to move on a short notice.' A little later he instructed a troop of Horse Artillery from Santa Barbara to move to Sumbilla.

Wellington was back at Lesaca in time for dinner at eight and approved the precautions that Murray had taken. Until further information arrived, he did not feel called upon to make further moves. Nor was the situation substantially changed by a report from Cole, written at one o'clock, which took more than eight hours to reach headquarters. This announced that Byng had been attacked in the Roncesvalles pass but that he was holding his own. Still believing that Soult's main thrust would be directed on San Sebastian, Wellington wrote to Graham before going to bed instructing him to re-embark the bulk of the siege material which would be an encumbrance in manœuvring the army. Reports so far accounted for only a small proportion of the French army: 'It is impossible to judge of Soult's plan yet . . . . One can hardly believe that, with 30,000 men, he proposes to force himself through the passes of the mountains. The remainder of his force, one would think, must come into operation on some other point, either tomorrow or the day after; and it is desirable that you should be prepared.' He also sent orders for one of the two Spanish divisions blockading Pamplona to move north to support Picton and Cole and for the cavalry to move up to Pamplona.

He was roused in the small hours by an aide-de-camp from General Hill. The news he brought was disturbing. There had been desperate fighting throughout the day on the Maya pass and although at evening the Second Division, which had had the assistance of three battalions from the Seventh, was still in a position to stop d'Erlon debouching from the pass, Hill had 'judged it advisable to retire' and was taking up a position to cover Elizondo. There was still no news from Cole.

Orders were at once despatched to meet the new threat. The Sixth Division was to send two of its brigades to touch in on Hill's new position. The third brigade was to remain in Santesteban, to secure that town which was vital for any movement of troops, French or Allied from the Baztan front to the Bidassoa. The Seventh Division was to march to Sumbilla where it would be closely in touch with the Sixth. 'The Light Division will place itself on the left bank of the Bidassoa, in such a situation as to be able to move by its right to St. Estavan or by its left towards Yanci and Lesaca.' The line of the Bidassoa was left to the care of the Spaniards.

Having made these dispositions, Wellington, at four in the morning, rode over to the valley of the Baztan where he found Hill strongly posted with 9,000 men in hand and no contact with the French, who had not followed up his retreat. He learned that in the previous day's fighting the Second Division had lost 1,300 men and four guns and that the situation had at one time been so serious that the two British brigades must have been driven in disorder from the pass, had not Major-General Barnes led two battalions of the Seventh Division in a desperate and wholly unexpected charge on to the French flank. This was so successful that the leading French troops fell back in disorder and the day's fighting had come to a standstill.

Finding Hill in no immediate danger, Wellington rode on towards his right flank from which he had received no news. Before evening he had reached Almandoz near the crest of the Col de Velate, where he intended to set up his headquarters. As a precautionary measure he ordered the Sixth Division to march on the following morning towards Pamplona, while the Seventh was to take over their post on Hill's left. About eight o'clock the long-awaited despatch reached him from Cole. This was a depressing document. Two British and one Portuguese brigades had defended the Pass of Roncesvalles and the Lindus plateau throughout the day. Their casualties had not been heavy, little more than 300, and they had not yielded an inch of ground. Cole, however, was over-burdened by the weight of responsibility and worry by musketry in his right rear, which was in fact nothing more than a diversion by the National Guards which was easily kept in check by his Spanish flank-guard. Although during the battle he had received orders from Murray which said, 'Lord Wellington has desired that I should express still more strongly how essential he considers it that the passes in front of Roncesvalles should be maintained to the utmost', the strain was too much for him. He gave orders for a retreat during the night on Picton's division near Zubiri. From his despatch it is clear that he was anxious to rid himself of responsibility by placing his division under the orders of Picton, his senior, and the state of his mind could be judged from his references to continuing his retreat beyond Pamplona towards Vitoria.

If things were going badly on the Allied side, they were scarcely better on the French. Soult had based his plan on surprise and on his ability to get to Pamplona before Wellington could bring his reserves across from his left and centre. Every hour was precious to him. Not only would his numerical superiority disappear as the days passed, but at the most generous calculation the French troops had rations only until the 29th and the foot-hills of the Pyrenees were not good country for foraging. Soult had accompanied the columns of Clausel and Reille on the left of the attack and had been forced to stand helplessly by while his corps commanders with overwhelming numbers were fought to a standstill by three allied brigades at Roncesvalles and the Lindus. Numbers were useless there as the way was too narrow to allow deployment. When, on the morning of the 26th, he found that Cole had left his position he ordered the advance to continue in two columns, again consigning Reille to a goat-track while Clausel marched along the main road. Reille, with Basque guides and no interpreter, became hopelessly lost in a fog on the heights and was forced to bring his divisions down on to the main road in rear of Clausel's. Nor was Soult's hope of keeping to his time-table increased by the fact that Cole's rearguard held up the French advance at Linzoain until dark on the 26th. Two days had gone and his leading troops were less than half-way from the pass to Pamplona.

From his right he heard nothing. For his peace of mind this may have been for the best, for d'Erlon, having found himself in possession of the Maya on the morning of the 26th, wasted the whole of that day in guarding against an imaginary threat to his right, and only made contact with Hill's outposts near Elizondo that evening. The total French loss in the battles of the 25th had been slightly above 2,500, of which more than four-fifths had been suffered in d'Erlon's attempt to force the Maya.

Picton's retreat to the outskirts of Pamplona left the right flank of Hill's corps guarded only by the hills of the Sierra de Aralar and since he was confronted by 18,000 men it was essential that he retire towards the Pass

Joseph Bonaparte, King of Spain by François Gérard

Jean-Baptiste Jourdan from an engraving
by H.R. Cook

Jean-de-Dieu Soult, Duc de Dalmatie
from an engraving by P. Cassairt after a
drawing by M.T. de Noireterre

'March of Baggage following the Army, 16th May 1811' from an aquatint by C. Turner after a watercolour by Major T. St. Clair

'A halt in the Pyrenees, July 1813' from an aquatint by J.C. Stadler after a drawing by W. Heath

The Battle of Salamanca, 22nd July 1813 from an engraving by J. Clark and M. Dubourg after a drawing by W. Heath

The Battle of the Bidassoa, 9th October 1813 from an engraving by D. Havell after a drawing by W. Heath

The Battle of the Nivelle, 10th November 1813 from an engraving by T. Sutherland after a drawing by W. Heath

'Attack on the road to Bayonne' The Battle of the Nive from an engraving by T. Sutherland after a drawing by W. Heath

of Velate. The Seventh Division would have to conform and must cross the Sierra by the passes of Dona Maria. Wellington gave these orders while he was riding towards Pamplona on the morning of 28th July. Although no message had been received from Picton, definite news that he had retreated from Linzoain came to Wellington when he reached Ostiz. Leaving Murray to hurry on the Sixth Division, he rode off at speed to join Picton. So fast did he ride that before he reached his position all the staff, except Lord Fitzroy Somerset, were left behind.

The main part of the position which Picton and Cole had chosen for a stand to cover the investment of Pamplona was a sharp ridge about four miles to the north of the town with the village of Sorauren below its western end. The ridge was about a mile and a half long and was covered on each flank by a small but swiftly flowing river. This part of the front was garrisoned by the three brigades of the Fourth Division with Byng's British brigade, Campbell's brigade from d'Amaranthe's division and two Spanish battalions. Picton's division was thrown back about a mile to another ridge and two Spanish divisions were aligned with him on high ground just out of range of the guns of Pamplona. It was a very powerful fighting-ground having only the disadvantage that it was just too far to the rear to cover the road to Ostiz, the most direct line of approach for reinforcements. It was by this road that Wellington was approaching.

He came in sight of the ridge just as the French were beginning to appear on the opposing height. 'It was rather alarming, certainly', he said afterwards, 'and it was a close run thing. When I came to the bridge at Sorauren, I saw the French on the hills, on one side, and it was clear that we could make a stand on the other hills; but I found that we could not keep Sorauren, for it was exposed to their fire and not to ours. I determined to take [up] the position, but was obliged to write my orders accordingly at Sorauren, to be sent back instantly, for had they not been dispatched back directly by the way I had come, I must have sent four leagues round. I stopped, therefore, to write accordingly, people saying to me all the time, "The French are coming! The French are coming!" I looked pretty sharp after them, however, every now and then, until I had completed my orders, and then set off, and I saw them just near one end of the village as I went out at the other end.'

Lord Fitzroy dashed out of the north end of the village under the noses of the French dragoons, carrying back to Murray orders for the Sixth Division to move by a safe but circuitous route to the left flank of the Sorauren position which they should reach by the following morning. The Second and Seventh Divisions were to move towards Lanz and Lizaso respectively.

Wellington, wearing a plain grey frock-coat buttoned to the neck and a plain cocked hat with an oilskin cover, rode alone up the western end of the Sorauren ridge. 'One of Campbell's Portuguese battalions first descried him and raised a joyful cry; then the shrill clamour, caught up by the next regiments, soon swelled as it ran along the line into that stern appalling shout which the British soldier is wont to give upon the edge of battle.'

Soult did not attack that afternoon. Only Causel's three divisions had reached the front and although their corps commander besought Soult to allow him to go forward, Soult preferred to take his luncheon and follow it with a short sleep while he waited for the head of Reille's corps to arrive. All that occurred that day was a sharp action on the Allied right when a French regiment tried to dispossess two Spanish battalions of a projecting spur and were firmly repulsed.

It was after midday on 28th July that the French advanced against the ridge. By that time the leading troops of the Sixth Division were on the ground and Soult was forced to detach a force to hold them in check. Nevertheless, 20,000 men were available to attack the 11,000 holding the ridge. 'The enemy', wrote Wellington to Graham, later in the day, 'were repulsed at every point with considerable loss. We have also lost a considerable number of men, particularly among the Fusiliers and the 4th Portuguese; the latter gave way, and the enemy broke through our line, which principally occasioned the loss of the Fusiliers; but upon the whole I never saw the troops behave so well.'

The next day was the last on which rations were available for the French army. Soult had been fought to a standstill and since reinforcements for Wellington were arriving it was clear that he could no longer hope to relieve Pamplona. He was equally certain that his reputation would not stand an ignominious retreat by the way he had come, and he resolved to attempt a new move which was so improbable that it must be doubtful whether he was altogether serious when he put it to his corps commanders. Having, on the morning of the 29th, made contact with d'Erlon's advance cavalry and learning that the main body of that corps was at Lanz he determined to turn westward, make d'Erlon's corps his advance-guard and try to relieve San Sebastian. This presupposed that the corps of Clausel and Reille could march across Wellington's front within artillery range and that the French army could fight its way to the coast without rations.

By the morning of 30th July Wellington had been joined by the Seventh Division who held the extreme left beyond Sorauren. At dawn the whole army were standing to their arms and as soon as it was light saw the French army struggling off to their right. The bulk of Clausel's corps had moved on to the Ostiz road during the night and although warmly assailed by the Seventh Division managed to continue its retreat in good order. They were more fortunate than the divisions which were still opposite Sorauren. Two divisions which had been detailed to hold the village of Sorauren while the remainder of the army filed across their rear, were almost destroyed. Another division, the final rear-guard, was so harassed by the Third and Fourth Divisions that it was forced to retreat eccentrically by the Pass of Aldudes carrying with it a mass of stragglers from other divisions. It can have been little consolation to Soult that on the same day d'Erlon with 18,000 men attacked Hill with half that number near Lizaso and drove him back a short distance. The fact remained that Reille's corps was a wreck and Clausel's was little better. Nevertheless, although the relief of San Sebastian was clearly out of the question, he still refused to retreat by the most obvious way, the Pass of Maya. He decided to strike across to the Bidassoa and fall back into France by the Pass of Echalar.

The improbability of this plan confounded Wellington who assumed that Soult would retire through the Maya rather than commit his battered army to the Santesteban-Yanci road which runs along the narrow defile of the Bidassoa. The bulk of the Allied pursuit was directed into the Baztan, but the Fourth Division hung on to the French rear inflicting damage all the way. The vital bridge at Yanci was in charge of Longa's Cantabrians. The Light Division had been sent to Lecumberri on the road from Pamplona to San Sebastian to maintain touch between Graham's corps and the main body. The orders to recall them miscarried and it was not until late in the evening of the 31st that orders reached them to return to the Bidassoa. By midday on the 1st they had covered 26 miles to Santesteban but, finding that the enemy were for the most part through that village, General Alten decided to take his leading brigade, which was somewhat less tired, and push on to the bridge of Yanci, which they reached in time to inflict terrible damage to the rear French division, trapped on the road between the river and a line of steep cliffs.

Next day a brisk attack by the Seventh and Light Divisions drove the French rear-guard over the Pass of Echalar and Soult's attempt to relieve Pamplona had finally failed. The loss to the French army was more than 13,000 men.

A month later, on 31st August, Soult made a last attempt to relieve San Sebastian. Seven divisions, 45,000 men, crossed the Bidassoa between Irun and Vera covered by a thick morning mist. On their right Reille with his own three divisions and the Reserve tried to drive the Spanish divisions from the heights of San Marcial. It was the greatest Spanish success since Baylen. The Spanish commander, Friere, following

Wellington's example, kept his men under cover until the French were almost upon him. Then the Spaniards gave a volley and charged. The French broke and fled down to the river. When the attack was renewed the same result followed. At one point the French reached the crest and Friere sent to Wellington for British reinforcements. Wellington refused. 'If I send you British troops, it would be said that they had won the battle. You may as well win it by yourselves.' The French loss in this attack was little short of 2,500 men.

The left-hand French column, three divisions under Clausel, fought an inconclusive action with three Allied brigades and gained some ground before a message from Soult recalled them after the failure of the frontal attack on the right. As the message arrived a great storm broke and the level of the Bidassoa rose with terrible rapidity. Before the French rear-guard was across there was six feet of water in the fords and four French brigades were on the southern bank. The only divisional commander present, Vandermaesen, decided that their only chance was to force a way across the bridge of Vera. The bridge was held by two weak companies of the 95th, but the whole of Skerrett's brigade was within easy supporting distance. Confident of support, the Riflemen clung to their post, but Skerrett, whom his Brigade Major described as being 'as stupidly composed for himself as inactive for the welfare of his command', refused to send any help, and the two companies were at last forced to retire leaving the French retreat open. Sixty-one of the hundred Riflemen at the bridge were casualties. The French loss was almost 500 men, Vandermaesen being killed. General Skerrett left for England soon afterwards on sick leave 'as his father was just dead, and he was heir to an immense fortune'.

The fighting on that day brought the French 3,800 casualties as against 2,500 on the Allied side. The only tangible gain was the capture of the British Judge Advocate General★ who was courteously returned a few weeks later. Even had the attack succeeded it would have been too late. San Sebastian was stormed that morning.

The siege of San Sebastian was not a very creditable operation. Chiefly at fault were the Engineers whose advice on the scheme to be followed was imperfect. The problem was a very difficult one. San Sebastian stands on a peninsula with the sea to the west and the estuary of the Urumea river on the east. It was decided to carry on the principal battering across the estuary and to assault the river front at low tide from the sand-hills which connect the town to the mainland, thus having the fire of the land

★ F. S. Larpent.

front of the walls pouring down into the flank of the storming-parties. The first assault, on 25th July, failed with 570 casualties. The upshot was fierce recriminations between the Engineers, who claimed that the infantry had not attacked with enough determination, and the Fifth Division who blamed the sappers for sending them to certain death. As a result Wellington called for volunteers from the First, Fourth and Light Divisions, 'who will show the Fifth Division that they have not been called upon to perform what is impractical'.

During the week of the battles of the Pyrenees the bulk of the siege-train was embarked for safety and the delay in landing the guns again, together with the fact that the navy did not manage to bring a new supply of ammunition until 23rd August, much delayed the renewal of the siege and gave the French commander, General Rey, a very determined officer, a chance to strengthen his defences.

The final assault, on the morning of 31st August, started badly. The Fifth Division's storming-parties were halted by heavy fire at the foot of the breach, and a gallant attack by a Portuguese brigade launched across the estuary over the open sands and through three feet of water in the river at low tide was equally unsuccessful. The volunteers from the other divisions were then sent forward and found 'the men of the 5th division were making no progress, but rather were crouching under cover of the fallen; we tried in vain to rouse them, and seeing a little to our right some men making head we moved towards them'. At this moment General Graham took an unprecedented step. He ordered the heavy batteries to open fire at the walls, just above the heads of the stormers. For a moment the stormers were aghast. 'A cry arose to come away as our batteries had opened on us.' Then they came forward and seized the breach which the guns had swept clear of defenders. By mid-afternoon the town was in Allied hands and the remnants of the garrison had taken shelter in the castle at the end of the peninsula in which they held out for a further week. The storm had cost the attackers 2,376 casualties, more than a third of whom were killed. There followed an orgy of looting, drunkenness and rape which surpassed even the sack of Badajoz.

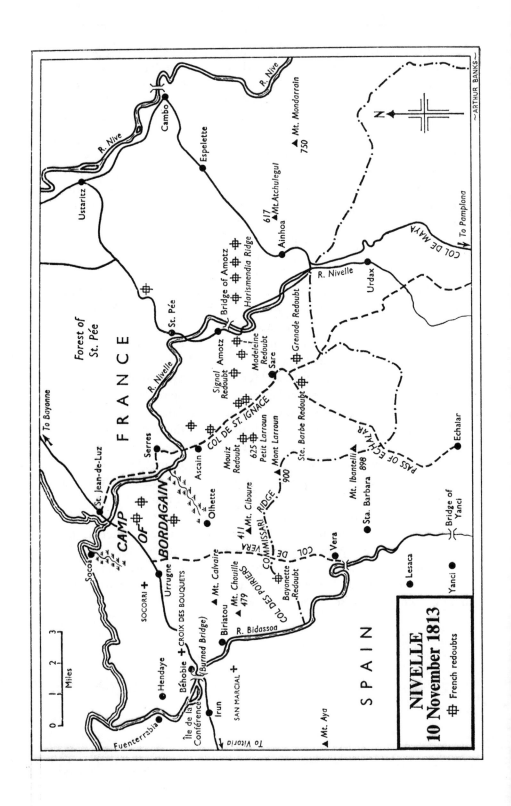

~ARTHUR BANKS~

R. Nive

Cambo

Espelette

R. Nive

▲ Mt. Mondarrain
750

Ustaritz

▲Mt.Atchulegul
617

Ainhoa

N

To Pamplona

COL DE MAYA

To Bayonne

Forest of
St. Pée

F R A N C E

St. Pée

R. Nivelle

Bridge of Amotz

Harismendia Ridge

R. Nivelle

Urdax

Grenade Redoubt

Signal

Amotz

Madeleine
Redoubt

Sare

Serres

Ascain

COL DE ST. IGNACE

Mouiz
Redoubt

Petit Larroun
625

Mont Larroun
900

Ste. Barbe Redoubt

PASS OF ECHALAR

Echalar

Signal
Redoubt

Olhette

Mt. Ciboure

411

Mt.

COMMISSARI RIDGE

Mt. Ibantelli
898

St. Jean-de-Luz

CAMP OF BORDAGAIN

Urrugne

SOCORRI

CROIX DES BOUQUETS

Mt. Calvaire ▲

Mt. Chouille
479 ▲

Biriatou ▲

COL DE POIRIERES

COL DE VERA

Bayonette
Redoubt

Vera

Sta. Barbara

Bridge of
Yanci

Lesaca

Yanci

Socoa

Miles

Hendaye

Béhobie

(Burned Bridge)

Île de la
Conférence

SAN MARCIAL

Irun

R. Bidassoa

Fuenterrabia

To Vitoria

▲ Mt. Aya

S P A I N

NIVELLE
10 November 1813

⊕ French redoubts

0 1 2 3

11

Nivelle – 10th November 1813

Less than a week after the fall of San Sebastian Wellington learned that
the armistice in the east had been ended and that Austria had joined the
coalition against Napoleon. Although Pamplona still held out, Wellington had 'every reason to hope that the place will be under the necessity
of surrendering early in October'. He was therefore ready to make a
limited advance into France. He was not anxious to do so. He wrote to
the Secretary of State on 19th October, 'I confess that I feel a great
disinclination to enter France under existing circumstances'. The
circumstances that led to his reluctance were many. The situation in
eastern Spain was more than usually gloomy. General John Murray,
whose task it had been to engage Suchet's attention by laying siege to
Tarragona during the Vitoria campaign, was to be court-martialled for
incompetence and worse. His successor had decided to return to Sicily
leaving the Anglo-Sicilian force under the command of a general of
whom he wrote 'diffidence makes him unfit for command; his fear of
responsibility and the anxiety and uneasiness he suffers under it would, I
am sure, in a very short time, ruin his constitution'. The possibility that
Suchet might take a hand in the main campaigns in Spain had always
worried Wellington and now that the Allied right flank had moved so
close to the Marshal's sphere of operations he was more than ever anxious
that Suchet's attention should be firmly held in his own area. Scarcely less
worrying was the behaviour of the Spanish authorities. Wellington had
never hoped for much positive benefit from his appointment as
Generalissimo of the Spanish armies and was little surprised when the
Government refused to accept his recommendations for promotion, or
when they posted away generals that he wished to keep, replacing them
with others whose services he did not greatly value. What he did resent
was the refusal of the Spanish authorities to feed their soldiers. There were
tens of thousands of troops in Spain who could not be employed because
neither food nor pay was ever sent to them, and those who were in the
front line were largely kept alive by issuing to them rations intended for
British and Portuguese troops. This was all the more disappointing since
San Marcial had shown the quality of the Spanish troops when properly
led, and Wellington reported that their conduct 'was equal to that of any

troops that I have ever seen engaged'. Nor were reports of the fighting in eastern Europe either clear or encouraging. News had been received of Napoleon's victory at Dresden but little was known of the compensating disasters at Kulm and Katzbach.

Nevertheless, Wellington gave the preliminary orders for an advance during the second week in September. His objective was strictly limited. He intended to gain the heights on the French bank of the Bidassoa which overlooked the Allied positions on the south bank. The strengths of the opposing armies were curiously equal. Leaving aside the cavalry who were quite useless in the kind of country which lay ahead, both the French field army and the Anglo–Portuguese force totalled, to within a few score, 61,500 infantry, artillery and engineers. 'The superiority of numbers which I can take into France consists in about 25,000 Spaniards, neither paid nor fed, and who must plunder, and will set the whole country against us.' With such a narrow and unreliable margin of superiority for an assault of a position naturally powerful, it was vital that every advantage from surprise should be used, and Wellington was careful to keep Soult's attention turned to sectors in which the Allies did not intend to attack. Although orders from Paris and Dresden were constantly urging him to take the offensive, Soult utterly refused to do so. Three times in three months the French army had been hunted over the French frontier and their morale had suffered accordingly. In an attempt to give his men back some confidence in themselves he determined to put as many of them as possible in fortifications and the whole army set to work with much civilian assistance to raise three fortified lines between the Bidassoa and Bayonne. The first line followed the course of the Franco–Spanish frontier, up the course of the river to Endarlaza and thence eastward to the great mountain complex of Mont Larroun (La Rhune), from where it continued on the French side of the passes of Echalar, Maya, Les Aldudes, and Roncesvalles. The second line had at its seaward end St. Jean-de-Luz and followed the course of the river Nivelle as far as Ascain. From there it swung south to the feature known as Petit Larroun* and thence eastward to the Mondarrain massif. The third line consisted of heavy local defences around the southern approaches of Bayonne itself, and followed the course of the River Nive.

In the first line, Soult devoted the main bulk of his force to his left and centre. On the left d'Erlon with four divisions, including one borrowed from Reille's corps, held the ground from St. Jean-Pied-de-Port to the

---

* The Petit Larroun referred to in all contemporary accounts of this fghting is not the height marked by that name on modern French maps, but Monte Alchangue.

Nivelle in the area of Ainhoa. The centre, from the Nivelle up to and including the Larroun massif was entrusted to Clausel's three divisions. The seaward sector, along the lower Bidassoa was guarded by the two divisions which remained in Reille's corps after one had been detached to d'Erlon's command on the left. The Reserve Division, 8,000 men strong under Villatte, was stationed around Ascain behind the right centre of the line.

Wellington ordered attacks in two sectors. Opposite the Larroun mountain, the force employed was to consist of the Light Division, Longa's Cantabrians and two weak divisions of the Army of Reserve of Andalusia under General Giron. The Larroun itself was to be the objective of the Andalusians while the Light Division and Longa's men were to seize the high ground to the west, above Vera. Four further divisions were ready behind the attackers to deal with any interference from the French left.

The main weight of the attack was to fall in the seaward sector. In the short stretch between Biriatou and the sea, the troops detailed to cross were the First and Fifth Anglo-Portuguese Divisions, two Spanish divisions and an independent Portuguese brigade. Two further independent brigades, one British and one Portuguese, formed the reserve. The whole force numbered about 24,000 men.

To oppose this attack were two French divisions, those of Maucune and Boyer. The stronger division, Boyer's, with 6,500 infantry, was held in the rear at Urrugne where most of its men were engaged in helping to construct works covering St. Jean-de-Luz. The force near the river consisted of only ten battalions, five of them spread along the bank between Hendaye and Endarlaza, a front of six miles as the river runs. The five remaining battalions were held back, four of them on the high ground between the Croix des Bouquets and Mont Calvaire. There was no bridge across this stretch of the river since the French had destroyed that of Béhobie in their retreat in June, and although there were a number of fords known between the Île de Conférence and Biriatou, neither Soult nor Reille who commanded this sector, expected any serious attack across the river. Below the Île de Conférence the river was reckoned impassable since at high tide it was up to 1,000 yards wide and 20 feet deep. The fact that it was in places fordable at low tide was known only to a few Basque shrimpers, and, after mid-September, to Wellington.

Wellington had hoped to attack on 23rd September, the day on which the tides would be at their lowest, but the Engineer responsible for the pontoon-train, which had been left at Vitoria, had failed to bring it forward. Wellington wrote, in deep disgust, on 17th September, 'he is not certain that the orders he sent have reached the officers in charge of them, and he has taken no measures to repeat them. He put his letter into the Spanish post office, I conclude directed in English, and without knowing whether the officer in charge of the pontoons is in communication with that post office.' The attack had to be postponed until 7th October.

Soult was convinced that Wellington's attack would come in the inland sector of his line and in this belief he was deliberately encouraged. Wellington arranged for much activity by patrols and skirmishers at that end of the front. In one operation a Portuguese brigade was sent out from the Aldudes passes and returned triumphantly with a French piquet and 2,000 sheep. Soult was much impressed and undertook a tour of inspection of St. Jean-Pied-de-Port and Espelette. More demonstrations were arranged for the morning of 7th October. These were so successful that Soult spent the early part of the day watching the Sixth Division manœuvring around Ainhoa and only reached the scene of the real fighting when it was over.

Shortly after 7.15 a.m. on 7th October the Fifth Division emerged from Fuenterrabia and dashed into the river. The water was 'middle deep so that the men had to hold up their arms and ammunition'. Only scattered shots opposed them as they doubled across the wide estuary and tumbled a piquet of 40 men out of Hendaye.

Simultaneously the First Division and the Spaniards emerged from their hiding-places in the foot-hills of the San Marcial feature, and, with their light companies leading, entered the river on a three-mile front upstream from the Île de Conférence. There was a little fighting in and above the village of Biriatou but the attacking forces were so large and advanced on such a wide front that the handful of French battalions could not hold for long without being surrounded. Only on the Croix des Bouquets ridge did they attempt a stand, reinforced by a single battalion from the rear division of the corps. It could not last, The First Division surged up the front of the ridge while the Fifth swung to their right and drove along the crest on to the French flank. Meanwhile the Spaniards had seized the Col des Poitiers and soon after noon the forward troops of the Allies were disputing the line Socorri-Urrugne-Olhette. At this point Wellington called the battle off. The whole line of high ground had been taken at the cost of no more than 400 casualties and there could be no justification for attempting to storm the fortifications around St. Jean-de-Luz out of hand with troops who had already achieved so much.

Further inland the fighting was more severe. Taupin's division held a spur running westward from the Larroun, known as the Commissari ridge. From it to the south ran two further spurs, both pointing at the village of Vera. Between them lay a wooded re-entrant up which ran the road from Vera to the north, crossing the ridge at the Col de Vera. The southern end of the re-entrant was blocked by a rounded hill, known to the British as 'The Hog's Back'. This was occupied by five companies. Both the south-pointing spurs were entrenched and the more westerly, the Bayonette spur, had solid works both at its southern eminence and near the junction with the Commissari ridge. To attack this formidable position, General Charles von Alten, the Hanoverian commander of the Light Division, had his own division and Longa's four battalions. Two of these last were, on Wellington's orders, used as a guard on the left flank, while the others were ordered to advance up the re-entrant while the brigades of the Light Division tackled the two projecting spurs.

The first necessity was the capture of the Hog's Back, which was entrusted to five companies of the Rifles. 'About twenty men, with twenty supporting, marched coolly up the hill, when the French who delight in a long shot, began firing the moment that our men showed their heads. However, the 95th moved regularly up the hill to within thirty yards of the top, without firing, and then by way of breathing gave a volley, loaded, and advanced to the top, the support just behind them. The French did not attempt to defend it, but moved to their left, in quick time.'

This success opened the way for Kempt's brigade to advance up the eastern spur, outflanking the French entrenchments as they climbed. The difficulties they encountered were more natural than human. 'The obstacles on each side of the way rendered the mountain fearfully difficult of ascent; as it was indeed so intersected with rocks, trees, brushwood and briar, that our hands and limbs were pierced with thorns and the trousers were literally torn in shreds from off our legs.'

On the Bayonette spur, Colborne's brigade met heavier resistance. The brigade commander wrote 'There were two fortresses on an immensely steep hill one above the other. Below the lower one the hill divided into three tongues. I arranged that the Rifles and Caçadores should go first up the hills on the right and left as skirmishers, and the 52nd which was to attack, up the hill in the centre. I arranged the attack in this manner. I did not allow the piquet to be relieved in the usual manner at daybreak, but ordered them to march on and the columns to support them, so that they were actually in the town of Vera before the French had any suspicion that an attack was intended.

'The Rifles being the first to attack, the French mistook them for Portuguese Caçadores, and rushing out of the redoubt drove them back, so that they all came tumbling back on the 52nd . . . . . The adjutant of the 52nd was surprised to find we were so near the fort. "Why, Sir, we are close to the fort." "To be sure we are," I said, "and now we must charge." I then led the 52nd on to a most successful charge.'

Having stormed the first redoubt and reformed, the 52nd with a thick screen of Riflemen marched up the spur to the redoubt at its junction with the Commissari ridge. 'To our astonishment the enemy did not defend their well-constructed work as determinedly as we had anticipated. Although they stood behind their parapets until we were in the act of leaping on them, they then gave way, and we were almost mixed together, till they precipitated themselves into a ravine and fled.'

On the right of the Light Division, Giron's Spanish division drove the enemy from the ridge which links the Commissari ridge to the Larroun, but they were repulsed from the rocky cone that forms the summit of the mountain. This however was of no consequence as the French garrison evacuated the position of their own accord on the following day. The operation in the centre had cost the Allies about 1,000 men, 370 of them in the Light Division, and the remainder in Giron's attempts to storm the summit of Mont Larroun. Thus with a loss of only 1,500 the whole of the left and left centre of Soult's first line were in Wellington's hands.

There was a pause lasting a month after the crossing of the Bidassoa. Wellington was not anxious to commit himself to a full-scale invasion of France until he was certain that conditions were wholly favourable. He had the constant fear that the arrival of a foreign army might provoke in France the kind of partisan resistance that the French had provoked in Spain and he knew that there was no chance that his force could ever be made up to a strength at which he could afford to detach large bodies of men to protect his lines of communication. His main concern was for the discipline of the troops. Although his British and Portuguese soldiers were capable of every kind of outrage, he believed that he could control them sufficiently to prevent them from raising the whole countryside against him. It was not possible to promise the same for the Spanish troops. Not only were they thirsting to revenge five years' maltreatment at the hands of the French but, since their government refused to feed them, they could only live by plunder.

Nor, throughout October, was the news from the eastern front encouraging. Always at the back of Wellington's mind was the fear that Russia, Austria and Prussia might conclude a separate peace with Napoleon and leave him free to turn his whole strength against the western Allies. Had he but known it, talks were held at the beginning of November with just such an object in view and only French intransigence caused them to fail.

The decisive factor was that Pamplona was not starved into surrender until 31st October, thereby releasing Spanish troops to hold the passes on the right wing and allowing the whole of the Anglo-Portuguese strength to be concentrated for a further advance.

Soult used the time for further fortifications. He was putting a bold front on his recent defeat, declaring that: 'Ultimately speaking, I consider the events of 7th October profitable to us, because the army is now more concentrated, and has its right wing resting in a much better position than before.' Advantageous or not, the surprise of his right wing had made a great impression on him and he was convinced that Wellington's next assault would fall in the seaward sector. The ground to the south of St. Jean-de-Luz was covered with fortifications and a very high proportion of his infantry was stationed there to the detriment of the rest of the line.

His position was naturally strong. His right flank was secured on the sea and the fortifications around the south of St. Jean, known as the armed camp of Bordagain. The left of the fortifications rested on the Nivelle, and both flanks were made impassable by flooding. Outside the lines, the village of Urrugne and the chapel of Socorri were held as strongpoints. The town of Ascain on the south bank of the Nivelle was held as a bridge-head, without fortification, while on the north bank, in the bend of the river, another armed camp was formed around the village of Serres.

Three miles to the south of Ascain, through very broken country was the Petit Larroun, itself a formidable fortification being a long narrow ridge presenting precipices on its southern and eastern faces and very steep slopes in the other directions. This height had been crowned by three redoubts and a further fort had been built on the plateau of Mouiz to the north. Eastward again there was a line of redoubts which stretched along a line of high ground to the Nivelle south of Amotz. These redoubts were in depth and in front of the line the village of Sare, the junction of the roads debouching from the passes of Maya and Echalar, was prepared for defence. To cover its southern approaches two redoubts, Ste. Barbe to the south and Grenade to the south-east were built.

On the east bank of the Nivelle, which is here flowing northwards before swinging in a great semi-circle round the northern foothills of the Larroun massif, the French line was continued by a series of redoubts along the crest of a steep narrow ridge which ends in the Mondarrain mountain, an obstacle at least as great as the Larroun. The eastern slopes of the Mondarrain fall sharply into the Nive river, which secured the left of the main French position. Further to the east was the fortified town of St. Jean-Pied-de-Port which had an adequate garrison, supported by a brigade of the Army of Aragon and a full division of Soult's army. Neither of these formations took any part in the main engagement.

Soult had 52,000 infantry available to hold the front between the sea and the Mondarrain. Twenty-five thousand of these were allocated to the sector between Ascain and the sea. Two divisions and the French and German brigades of the Reserve were stationed at the camp of Bordagain and a further division with the Italian and Spanish Reserve brigades held the camp of Serres, the Ascain bridge-head and two redoubts on the south bank of the Nivelle.

This westward concentration meant that the rest of the front was more lightly held. Clausel, with 16,000 men in three divisions, was assigned to the front between the Petit Larroun and the Nivelle at Amotz, while d'Erlon had only 11,000 men to hold the seven miles between the Nivelle and the Nive. Neither Clausel nor Reille could call on any reserves save those they set aside from their own inadequate resources.

Wellington had no intention of obliging Soult by attacking him in front of St. Jean-de-Luz. Not the least of the fruits of the victory of 7th October had been the splendid observation post made by the summit of the Larroun. From here every redoubt and trench in the French lines could be counted. He was a constant visitor to the Light Division outpost there. 'One day he stayed unusually long. He turns to Colborne, "These fellows think themselves invulnerable, but I will beat them out, and with great ease . . . ." "That we shall beat them", says Colborne, "when your lordship attacks, I have no doubt, but for the ease . . . ." "Ah, Colborne, with your local knowledge only, you are perfectly right; it appears difficult, but the enemy have not men to man the works and lines they occupy. They dare not concentrate a sufficient body to resist the attacks I shall make upon them. I can pour a greater force on certain points than they can concentrate to resist me." "Now I see it, my lord," says Colborne. The Duke was lying down, and began a very earnest conversation. General Alten, Kempt, Colborne and other staff officers were preparing to leave when he says, "Oh, lie still." After he had conversed for some time with Sir G. Murray, Murray took out of his sabretache his writing materials, and began to write the plan of attack for the whole army. When it was finished, so clearly had he understood the Duke, I do not think he erased one word. He says, "My lord, is this your desire?" As Murray read, the Duke's eye was directed with his telescope to the spot in question. He never asked Sir G. Murray one question, but the muscles of his face evinced lines of the deepest thought. When Sir G. Murray had finished, the Duke smiled and said, "Ah, Murray, this will put us in possession of the fellows' lines".'

The main attack was to be delivered between the village of Sare and the Nivelle. Here on a front of three miles, Sir William Beresford was to attack with the Third, Fourth and Seventh Divisions, 20,000 infantry. On their left, Giron, with more than 6,000 Andalusian infantry, was to operate on the eastern slopes of the Larroun towards the Col de St. Ignace. To the left of the Spaniards the Light Division was detailed to seize the Petit Larroun and then strike sideways at the flank of the line which

Beresford was assaulting frontally. On the right bank of the Nivelle, another strong corps was formed. Sir Rowland Hill, having handed over the pass of Roncesvalles, now snow-bound, to Spanish troops, commanded a further 20,000 men of the Second, Sixth and Portuguese divisions. These were to advance in echelon of divisions against the ridge held by d'Erlon's corps. The Sixth on the left was to lead with the Second Division taking the right, retarded, flank. Beyond them Morrillo's Spanish division acted as a flank-guard.

To keep Soult's over-weighted right wing from sending help to their colleagues on the left and centre, an impressive diversion was arranged. While four small ships of war demonstrated against Socoa and St. Jean-de-Luz, the First and Fifth Divisions and two independent brigades, 13,000 infantry, were to feign attack on the camp of Bordagain. This left corps was now commanded by Sir John Hope, Graham's eye-trouble having again forced him to apply for leave. Linking this demonstration with the operations on the Petit Larroun were three divisions of Spaniards whose objective was the Ascain bridge-head. Thus, while between the Larroun and the sea both sides brought about 20,000 men to a mock battle, between the Larroun and the Mondarrain, the French could only oppose 27,000 infantry to the 50,000 men of the corps of Beresford, Hill and Giron and the Light Division. A further 9,000 Frenchmen were stationed far out to the east around St. Jean-Pied-de-Port, which had an adequate garrison of its own and to which the approaches were all but impassable.

Wellington, not without reason, was supremely confident of the result. At dinner on 9th November, the evening before the battle, 'he was all gaiety and spirits, and only said on leaving the room, "Remember! At four in the morning".' Not only was he confident of his plan and of the fighting ability of his troops, but he had just received good news. Stories had come across from the French lines, that 'Bonaparte is beaten back to the Rhine, with the loss of three divisions'. The French army fought on the following day knowing that, on the eastern front, Napoleon had met with disaster at Leipzig.

The attack was ordered for daybreak, about quarter past six, and was to be signalled by the firing of a three-pounder mountain-gun from the summit of the Larroun. Long before this the troops had been moving up to their start-lines through a 'most beautiful moonlight morning; and so clear that it was difficult to say at what moment night ended and daylight began'. The preliminary tasks were the carrying of the Petit Larroun by the Light Division, of the Ste. Barbe redoubt by the Fourth and of the Grenade by the Third Division. In the deep shadows between the two Larrouns the Light Division had crept forward, navigating by bushes and rocks. At one moment a company was seen to be off course and heading straight for the French lines. 'About an hour before daylight, by some accident, a soldier's musket went off. It was a most anxious moment, for we thought the enemy had discovered us; but most fortunately all was still.'

Colborne's brigade was to swing round to the north of the mountain and seize the Mouiz redoubt while Kempt's had the task of storming the Petit Larroun itself. This storm was entrusted to the 43rd, commanded by William Napier. 'The plan of attack was entirely my own, for General Kempt wished me to attack the rocks with my whole battalion, and it was with difficulty I obtained his leave to detach Captain Murchison, to try the marsh on our left, and to keep down, if possible, the enemy's fire. A rifle sergeant sent to sound the marsh had assured the general it was impassable, but I was convinced it was not; and so it proved, for Murchison passed it, and contributed by his judgement and gallantry very much to the success of the attack; he was mortally wounded at the very moment of victory.

'I had a great distance to march on a front line towards the rocks and under fire, before I could gain the narrow entrance between the lower post and the marsh, where only the enemy could be attacked, for in the other parts the rocks were 200 feet high. There were two things to be principally looked to: first, not to blow the men by running too soon, and thus coming breathless to the stone castles which had been built up by the enemy, and would require great exertions of bodily strength as well as courage to face; secondly as the men were sure to be broken and dispersed by fighting among the rocks, and as they would be liable to disorders when they had carried them – for we knew nothing of the nature of the ground nor of the enemy's reserves behind the ridge – it was essential to have our reserves well in hand. In this view I placed four companies under Major Duffy at a distance of 300 yards, and with the four remaining companies advanced in person to storm the rocks. I had not, however, proceeded above half the distance when the fire became very heavy, and at this moment when I had the greatest difficulty to keep the men from breaking into a charge, the Hon. Captain Gore, A.D.C. to General Kempt, who looking down upon us from the heights could not see how rugged the ground was, nor judge of our distance, thinking us slow – with the impetuosity of a young staff officer rode down at full speed and galloped up behind my line, waving his hat, and shouted out to charge.

'The men immediately cheered and ran forward. In vain to try, and would have been dangerous, to stop them, and I could only make the best of the matter. I was the first man but one who reached and jumped into the rocks, and I was only second because my strength and speed were unequal to contend with the giant who got before me. He was the tallest and most active man in the regiment, and the day before, being sentenced to corporal punishment, I had pardoned him on the occasion of the approaching action. He now repaid me by striving always to place himself between me and the fire of the enemy. His name was Eccles, an Irishman; he died afterwards a sergeant and a pensioner on the Irish establishment.

'The mischief I had forseen now arrived; the men were quite blown and fell down among the rocks within a few yards of the first castle, from whence the enemy plied them with a heavy musketry. When they had recovered wind I advanced against the first castle: the enemy fled with the exception of an officer and two men; but aided by my own men I scaled the wall. We put the two men to flight and wounded and took the officer, for he fought to the last, standing on the wall and throwing heavy stones at me. One I parried with my sword, but I received a contusion on my thigh from another.

'The regiment then carried several castles in succession, the enemy fighting us muzzle to muzzle the whole way, so that many of the men's clothes were scorched all over the front with the fire. When I got to their principal place of arms, and had only one remaining castle called the Donjon to carry, I saw a breastwork entrenchment and fort below the ridge were still defended by the French and that they were very numerous. I therefore endeavoured to rally my companions, both to make a vigorous assault on the Donjon and to have a body in hand to attack the rear of those defending the entrenchment below. While thus employed, Lieut. Steele, a very quick and brave officer, called out that they were wavering in the Donjon; and as it was very strong and covered by a cleft in the rock fifteen foot deep, and only to be turned by one narrow path winding round the rock on the right, I gave up the notion of rallying the broken men, and rushing forward with what I had, carried the Donjon.'

Meanwhile Colborne's brigade had stormed the Mouiz redoubt and the whole Petit Larroun feature was in Allied hands. The Light Division then reformed on the Mouiz plateau and waited until the troops on their right had secured the village of Sare and were ready to attempt the main line of the French fortifications.

In front of Beresford's corps, the French put up a longer resistance. 'We attacked at daybreak,' wrote an artillery officer, 'opening with eighteen guns on the advanced redoubt [Ste. Barbe]. The enemy hastily withdrew his piquets, affording an opportunity for the horse artillery to gain the ridge on which the redoubt was, and to open within four hundred yards of it. It was not, however, till after an hour's firing, that the enemy seeing that our columns of infantry approached on all sides, abandoned a redoubt, made with every care, having a deep ditch, an abattis in front, and *trous de loup*. The next redoubt on the enemy's left [Grenade], against which we rapidly advanced our guns, cost only a quarter of an hour, the enemy abandoning it with discreditable precipitation. But by this time, though the ground was most difficult, the infantry were advancing with great celerity. One of those bursts of cheering, which electrify one, now indicated the presence of Lord Wellington. We advanced through rugged roads, and up and down heights more than difficult to the village of Sare.' There was a short stand around Sare, but the garrison seeing an overwhelming body of troops advancing towards them and hearing firing from Giron's Spaniards who were brushing away light opposition in the right rear of the village, did not stay to fight and by eight o'clock Clausel's corps was back on its main line of redoubts with two of his three divisions much shaken.

About an hour later, the whole Allied corps advanced again. On the right the Third Division stormed the Madeleine redoubt on a hill above the river and was able to throw its Portuguese across the bridge of Amotz, where it did much to discomfort those who were resisting Hill's corps on the right bank. There was sharp fighting to take the redoubts, but at the western end of the line near the Col de St. Ignace the Light Division struck in on the flank of the defenders. The 52nd, having scrambled down the precipitous north-eastern slope of the Petit Larroun and crossed a narrow stone bridge across a ravine enfiladed by four guns, formed up in a sunken road and charged home on the twin redoubts of St. Ignace. The garrison gave them a volley and fled. Pushing on north-eastward, the same battalion reached the Signal redoubt in the rear of the main French position. Owing to a misunderstanding of an order from General Alten, Colborne twice attempted to storm it out of hand. Both attempts failed. 'There was I', wrote Colborne, in later years, 'on top of this hill heading the 52nd, and exposed to a most murderous fire, the balls and shells falling like hailstones. My aide-de-camp, Captain Fane, dismounted and entreated me to do the same. "Pray get off, Sir, pray get off."

'I was never in such peril in my whole life, but thinking the boldest plan was the best, I waved my handkerchief and called out loudly to the French leader on the other side of the wall, "What nonsense this is, attempting to hold out! You see you are surrounded on every side. There are Spaniards on the left; you had better surrender at once!" (Frenchmen had a horror of falling into the hands of the Spaniards.) The French officer thought I was addressing his men and inciting them to surrender, which would have been very improper, and I ought not to have spoken so loud, but the danger was imminent and the moment critical . . . that the French should surrender was our only chance of escape. The French officer exclaimed, "*Vous parlez à mes hommes, je prévois un désastre*", meaning that

I and my regiment would be destroyed. However, I replied, "That is all nonsense; you must surrender! On this, the Frenchman appeared to hesitate, and finally asked me into the fort to arrange matters. There, with his pen in his hand, he pretended to be thinking of terms, but on my again repeating that it was nonsense, he surrendered at once with his regiment, the 88th.'

On the right bank of the Nivelle, Hill's troops overran d'Erlon's position without much trouble. The Sixth Division, with the river on their left flank, faced a stiff fire as they advanced up the steep ridge, but when they reached the crest the defenders broke and ran, seeing the Portuguese of the Third Division in their rear. Further to the east, the Second Division had to storm a single redoubt, which it achieved with only 150 casualties.

Soon after 2 p.m. the whole of Clausel's corps had struggled back to the north bank of the Nivelle by the bridges around St. Pée. The Allied light troops followed at their heels up to the river line. Wellington halted the main body of the attacking force on the high ground above the river to reform and to give time for the artillery to come forward. This last proved almost impossible and only a single troop of Horse Artillery was able to make its way through the rugged ground. It was not until nearly four o'clock that the order was given for the Third and Seventh Divisions to cross by the bridges downstream from St. Pée. 'The river is twenty or thirty yards wide, rapid, and not fordable', wrote the artillery officer previously quoted, 'After severe skirmishing, the troops crossed the bridges in three columns. The enemy had shown considerable bodies of troops on the heights on his side, which were of difficult access through vineyards, and were surmounted by woods. Ross's guns played on the enemy with visible effect, and just before dark the heights were carried.'

That night the French abandoned their fortifications around St. Jean-de-Luz and fell back on Bayonne and by the end of 11th November were established in some sort of order on the line of the Nive from Bayonne to Cambo. They had lost 4,350 men. Two thousand nine hundred of these, including 1,200 prisoners, came from Clausel's corps.

The Allied casualties amounted to rather more than 3,000, of which about 2,500 were British. The heaviest losses fell on the Third and Light Divisions, which lost respectively 500 and 450 men. The Fourth and Seventh each lost between three and four hundred. The demonstration in front of St. Jean-de-Luz which contented itself with seizing the outworks in Urrugne and Socorri cost 270 men, killed and wounded. When Hope's corps occupied the town and its defences they took 59 pieces of artillery and large quantities of military stores.

Soult had failed in his second attempt to hold the frontiers of France with a powerful army in a strongly fortified position and although there is no doubt that the French troops fought below their best form in the battles of the Bidassoa and the Nivelle there can equally be no doubt that on each occasion Soult was utterly outgeneralled and that his army would have been handsomely beaten even if it had been at the top of its form. After the Nivelle Wellington was through the mountain barrier which separates Spain from France and there was no natural obstacle in the way of his advance greater than the broad River Nive.

12

'The Vasty Fields of France'

On the night of the battle of the Nivelle, Wellington invited the commander of the 88me Régiment, captured that morning at the Signal redoubt, to dine with him. 'He came, but was very sulky. My staff were pressing him with questions, to which he gave no answers, or very dry ones. I, however, interfered quietly, and whispered to them to let him alone, and that after a good dinner and a few glasses of Madeira, our friend would mend. So in the course of the evening I saw he was in better humour, and then apologised for the fare I was obliged to give him, and still more for the apartment in which it was served . . . it was a wretched kind of barn: "But you", I said, "who have served all over the world, have probably been used to such things, and indeed your Emperor himself must of late had some hard nights' lodging himself; and, by the way", I added, "where was his *quartier-général*, when you last heard of him?" "*Monseigneur*", said our man with a tragic grimace, "*Il n'y a plus de quartier-général*". He alluded to the rout of Leipzig, and then I saw my way clearly to Bordeaux and Paris.'

Soult was given another month to do what he could to restore the morale of his army. The day after the Nivelle fighting the weather broke. Away from the main roads all movement became impossible. 'The infantry sank to the mid-leg, the cavalry to the horses' knees, and even to the saddle girths in some places: the artillery could not move at all.' The time was badly needed. The fighting spirit of the French was at a low ebb and their habits of pillage, acquired during their long years in Spain were losing them all sympathy and assistance from their compatriots. Courts martial sat incessantly and dealt out harsh sentences but indiscipline was scarcely checked. One division which had fought particularly poorly in the recent battle was broken up and used as reinforcements for the remaining eight divisions. Further, Soult decided that the plan which he had followed since the autumn of relying on a static defence in fortified lines would no longer serve. Instead of fortifying the crossings of the Nive, he merely watched the river line with light forces and hoped that his opponent would divide his army so that the French could defeat it in detail. Wellington was bound to take some such step if he was to make any further advance. Although he had broken through the mountain defences his army was still pinned in a small triangle. As a company commander wrote, 'with the sea on our left, the river Nive on our right and the lofty mountains of the Pyrenees at our backs – it may fairly be said that the army were in a *cul-de-sac*'.

Wellington had another very serious problem. On the night of 10th November his Spanish troops had indulged in an orgy of plunder, arson and violence in the town of Ascain. This finally decided him to send them back to their own country. He wrote to London: 'I despair of the Spaniards. They are in so miserable a state, that it is really hardly fair to expect that they will refrain from plundering a beautiful country, into which they enter as conquerors; particularly adverting to the miseries which their own country has suffered from its invaders. I cannot therefore venture to bring them into France, unless I can pay and feed them . . . . If I could now bring forward 20,000 good Spaniards, paid and fed, I should have Bayonne. If I could bring forward 40,000, I do not know where I should stop. Now I have both the 20,000 and the 40,000 at my command, upon this frontier, but I cannot venture to bring forward any for want of means of paying and supporting them. Without pay and food, they must plunder; and if they plunder they will ruin us all.' Immediately after Nivelle all the Spanish troops except Morillo's division of 4,500 men, which could be fed from British sources, returned to Spain. With them went a blistering letter, in which Wellington wrote, 'I am not invading France to plunder; thousands of officers and men have not been killed and wounded in order that the survivors might rob the French'.

The loss of the Spaniards meant that Wellington had sacrificed his numerical superiority. He could now put into the field, including Morillo's division, 63,500 men. Soult's field army, including the strong brigade which he had acquired from Suchet's army, and which now held his right wing about four miles upstream from Cambo, totalled 55,000 to which must be added the garrison of Bayonne, 8,800 strong, which was now in the front line against the Allies. Thus the opposing armies were almost exactly equal in numbers.*

Although the French had the advantage of a strong position, with their flank secured on a powerful fortress, the Allied army had an immeasurable superiority in morale, bred of uninterrupted victory and of confidence in their commander. 'The hardships and privations of the mountains had improved the quality of the troops. Fine air and the absence of drink had confirmed their health, while strict discipline and their own eagerness to

---

* The cavalry of both sides have been omitted from this calculation as they were, for the time being, useless.

enter the fair plains of France had excited their military qualities to a wonderful degree.' The result exceeded Wellington's highest expectations. 'The conduct of the British and Portuguese troops has been exactly what I wished; the natives of this part of the country are not only reconciled to the invasion, but wish us success, afford us all the supplies in their power, and exert themselves to get for us intelligence. In no part of Spain have we been better, I might say so well, received.'

Confident that his rear was secure Wellington waited only for suitable weather to send his right across the Nive. His opportunity came on 9th December. Five divisions crossed at Ustaritz and Cambo against only the lightest opposition and established their advanced posts in the angle between the Nive and Ardour rivers close up to the south-eastern defences of Bayonne.

This was the chance for which Soult had been waiting. Next morning he threw almost the whole strength of his held army against the Allied position between the Nive and the sea. His main thrust down the centre of the triangle achieved little beyond the surprise of some outposts. The Light Division, firmly ensconced in the church and château of Arcangues, gave no ground before the rather half-hearted onslaught of three divisions under Clausel. A subsidiary attack nearer the coast came much closer to success. Here, Sir John Hope had put his British and German brigades of the First and Fifth Divisions into billets, three and ten miles behind his outpost line and Reille, with two divisions, found himself opposed only by British and Portuguese piquets backed by two Portuguese brigades. The outposts were completely surprised, but a Portuguese brigade managed to stand in the buildings of Barrouillet until the first reinforcements arrived. Reinforcing success, the French diverted a division from their centre division to strengthen Reille and moved Villatte's Reserve to his support. This fresh onslaught almost forced the Barrouillet position by taking the defenders in flank, but at the crucial moment Lord Aylmer's brigade, having marched up the ten miles from St. Jean-de-Luz, fell, in turn, on the French flank and drove them back. The attack was not renewed and Hope did not attempt to press his belated advantage. At the end of the day Reille's men held the line on which the Allied piquets had been posted but had gained nothing more. The Allied loss had been more than 1,700, including 507 prisoners, the highest total of prisoners for any day in action during Wellington's command. Hope, who by his folly in disposing his troops, was responsible for the crisis, was twice slightly wounded and had several balls through his hat and coat.

The French casualties on this day cannot be exactly ascertained. Soult returned them as 'about one thousand' but he was notorious for his low estimates of his own losses. They were greatly increased by the desertion, that night, of three German battalions who marched over to the Allied lines, 1,400 strong.

Foiled on the left bank of the Nive, Soult countermarched with six divisions and on 13th December fell on Hill's corps stationed on the right bank on the heights above St. Pierre-d'Irube. Hill had available only 14,000 men of the Second and Portuguese Divisions. The troops which should have been ready to support him had been moved to assist in the fighting on the left bank and had not yet returned. Reinforcement was made more difficult by the flooding Nive which swept away the temporary bridge which Wellington had built at Villefranque. The fighting was as fierce as at Barrouillet and the situation was made more desperate by the cowardice of two British lieutenant-colonels, one of whom abandoned his battalion while the other ordered his to retreat, opening a wide gap in Hill's line. The defection of one of these, Nathaniel Peacock, who was found far to the rear beating a Portuguese mule-driver, caused even the mild-tempered Rowland Hill to express himself forcibly, the only time, apart from the night attack at Talavera, that such an occurrence was ever noted. When this reached Wellington's ears he is reported to have remarked, 'If Hill is beginning to swear we had better get out of the way'. By the time that Wellington with the leading reserves reached the battle-field, Hill had won the fight for himself, though at the cost of 1,700 casualties.

Although Soult had had the chance he hoped for and had been able to attack each wing of Wellington's army in succession with greatly superior force he had gained nothing but a few insignificant acres near the sea. His loss between 9th December when the Allied left crossed the river and his repulse four days later at St. Pierre amounted to more than 4,900 men. Over and above that there must be added the 1,400 men of the German battalions which came over to the Allies and another German battalion which failed to make good its escape and was disarmed by the French. Thus the total loss to the French was a little less than 7,000 men.

There followed a pause of two months while the weather made operations impossible and the two armies which had been continually on the move since early May found what comfort and rest they could from billets in the towns and villages of south-west France. Wellington wrote just before Christmas: 'Great anxiety is expressed in England that we should continue our operations; which I can promise only not to discontinue when the state of the roads will permit. But it does not appear possible at present to march troops by any road whatever.'

Before Wellington could move again, Soult's army was much reduced. To rebuild the army shattered at Leipzig, Napoleon had withdrawn from his lieutenant three cavalry brigades, two infantry divisions and five batteries. In addition the Italian brigade of the Reserve was sent to its native country to resist the Austrian advance, and the Spanish brigade was disbanded. The remaining field army consisted of only 38,000 infantry, 3,800 cavalry and 77 guns. Soult was promised a large number of newly raised conscripts but none of these very raw troops arrived until the campaign was lost.

Against this Wellington could bring 60,000 men of the Anglo-Portuguese army alone and he had beside made arrangements to provision a large number of Spanish troops with the reasonable hope that they would be amenable to discipline.

On 14th February the main body of the Allied army moved. Beresford with the Third, Fourth, Sixth, Seventh and Light Divisions marched due east driving the French before him, while Hill with his usual corps, the Second, and Portuguese Divisions with Morillo's Spaniards swung like a flail round the southern flank of the French, turning each of the river lines which they attempted to hold. Nine days later, Hope's corps with the support of a rocket troop, Royal Horse Artillery, crossed the wide and tidal mouth of the Adour below Bayonne and invested the city, into which Soult had thrown one of his field divisions making the garrison up to 15,000 men. The siege was never vigorously pressed and the garrison was still holding out when the war ended.

Soult with his remaining six divisions attempted a stand at Orthez on 27th February. The early part of the battle was hotly contested and Wellington's original plan failed, the Fourth Division being heavily repulsed. Committing almost his last reserve, Wellington broke through the strong French position just as Hill's column arrived and turned their left flank outside the main line. The French army fled to shelter behind the Luy de Béarn and their flight was only saved from becoming a rout because the three brigades of cavalry which pursued them were much hampered by the enclosed nature of the ground. Towards the end of the battle Wellington 'received a wound from a spent shot in the leg, which, although it did not prevent his continuing on horseback, confined him for a few days afterwards'.

A week later Beresford was despatched with the Seventh Division to seize Bordeaux, which he achieved with the active co-operation of the inhabitants on 12th March. The Seventh remained in the city for the rest of the war but Beresford returned to the main army which had been resting while the Bordeaux operation took place. On 18th March the advance started once more and, after a few sharp rear-guard actions Soult with his entire army marched into Toulouse on 24th March. The Allies followed him in a leisurely fashion.

The battle of Toulouse fought on Easter Sunday, 10th April 1814, was an unnecessary battle. The eastern Allies had entered Paris on 31st March and the Emperor had finally abdicated on 6th April. This news did not reach Wellington until two days after the battle. It was one of the most difficult operations that the Allied army ever undertook. Toulouse stands on the east bank of the Garonne, a river so broad that not only was an assault-crossing out of the question, but the Allies had much difficulty in bridging it well away from the enemy. The only permanent bridge into the city was covered by the fortified suburb of St. Cyprien, covered in turn by a line of entrenchments. One look at this front convinced Wellington that no progress could be made here without a heavy siege-train, which he did not have. The north and west faces of the city were covered by the Canal du Midi, a hundred yards wide. The only front not covered by an immediate obstacle was that to the south. It was from this direction that Wellington wished to make his attack, but two attempts to pass troops above the city across the Garonne failed because the pontoon-bridge carried with the army was 80 feet too short.*

There was no alternative but to cross the river below the city and to attack one of the faces protected by the canal. On the west bank there lies a 300 foot-high ridge, three miles long, which had been hastily fortified with redoubts and trenches. Possession of this ridge, known as Mont Rave, would make Toulouse untenable. It was, however, extremely difficult to assault. Between a mile and two miles beyond it flows the substantial River Ers. Much of the ground between the Ers and Mont Rave was marshy and impassable.

Toulouse was, in fact, a fortress and its garrison was Soult's entire army 42,000 strong, 35,000 of them infantry. Against them Wellington brought 50,000 men, of whom 40,000 were infantry, including 10,000 Spaniards. His plan was a bold, almost a foolhardy one. It was certainly one that could only be justified by success. On the west bank of the Garonne, Hill's corps were to demonstrate against the defences of St. Cyprien. The Third and Light Divisions were to make feints against the bridge-heads over the canal to the north of the town. The main attack on the Mont Rave was to be made in two sections. The northern end of the ridge was to be assaulted by two Spanish divisions while Beresford with the Fourth and Sixth Divisions was to make a hazardous approach march across the French front between the marsh and the ridge at the end of which he

---

* This infuriated Wellington, the more so since it was his own fault. He had been warned by the C.R.E., before leaving St. Jean-de-Luz, that the bridge would be too short for a large river, but disregarded the warning.

was to turn into line and attack the ridge between its centre and its southern end.

The day began badly. The Spaniards advanced too early . 'Although full half a mile away from the enemy', wrote an observer in the Light Division, 'they started in double quick time. "This," we said, "won't last long." They, however, drove the French from some entrenchments on the side of the hill, and continued to ascend till they reached the high road, which, being cut out of the side of the hill, afforded them shelter from the fire of the enemy. Here they came to a halt; and not all the endeavours of their officers, many of whom set a gallant example, could make them move a step further; the French perceiving this, after a little time sent down a strong body of *voltigeurs*, who, firing right among the Spaniards, sent them headlong down the hill. Our division immediately formed line, and the Spaniards, passing through the intervals, rallied in our rear. They looked much mortified by their defeat, and bore rather sulkily the taunts of our Portuguese, who were not sorry to have a wipe at their neighbours.' On the right of this failure Picton turned his demonstration against the canal bridge-heads into a serious attack. He was repulsed having incurred more than 400 needless casualties. A second assault by the Spaniards was also beaten back. But Beresford did not fail. Advancing up the steep face of the ridge, under heavy fire from the artillery and small arms, menaced at one time by cavalry, the Fourth and Sixth Divisions reached the crest and drove the French from the most southerly redoubts. Then they turned north and fought their way along the ridge. The Spaniards were launched on their third attack and reached the top to find that the enemy had retired into Toulouse.

The Allied loss was great, 4,500 men, of whom 2,000 were Spaniards, 1,500 in the Sixth Division and 400 in the Fourth. The French casualties amounted to 3,200 but that night the whole French army marched out of the city to the south.

On the evening of the 12th just as Wellington was sitting down to dinner a British and a French officer rode in from Paris with the news of the Emperor's abdication and of the restoration of the Bourbons. 'The whole was out directly, champagne went round, and after dinner Lord Wellington gave "Louis XVIII" which was very cordially received with three times three, and white cockades were ordered for us to wear at the theatre that evening. In the interim, however, General Alava got up and gave Lord Wellington's health as the *Liberador del Espagna!* Every one jumped up and there was a sort of general exclamation from all the foreigners . . . French, Spanish, Portuguese, Germans and all . . . *El Liberador d'Espagna! Liberador de Portugal! Le Libérateur de la France! Le Libérateur de l'Europe!* And this was followed not by a regular three times three, but a cheering all in confusion for nearly ten minutes! Lord Wellington bowed, confused, and immediately called for coffee. He must have been not a little gratified with what had passed.'

APPENDIX I

A Note on Weapons

Since all successful tactics are based on the weapons used, a note on the arms used in the Peninsular war may help to explain the battles described in these pages.

The dominant weapon on both sides was the infantryman's musket. In the British and Portuguese army, and increasingly in the Spanish, the infantry of the line were armed with the 'East India' pattern musket; a modification of 'Brown Bess', the standard British musket since the end of Marlborough's wars. This had a smooth-bore barrel 39 inches long and a flint-lock action. The bore was 0.75 inch and it threw a ball weighing rather more than an ounce ($14\frac{1}{2}$ to the pound). Although the ball would be lethal up to 300 yards, even the most expert shot could not reckon on hitting a target at more than 80 yards. A contemporary writer remarked that, 'a soldier must be very unfortunate indeed who shall be wounded by a common musket at 150 yards, provided that his antagonist aims at him'. The rate of misfires was as high as 2 in 13 even in fine weather, and in rain it was unlikely that any shots could be fired at all. A trained soldier could reload and fire in between 12 and 15 seconds. During this time he was defenceless except for his bayonet. The French musket was comparable in performance, but threw a slightly lighter ball, 20 to the pound.

Armed with such weapons both sides were compelled to fight in close order. Only by forming up shoulder to shoulder and firing in closely controlled volleys, either by ranks or by files, could a sufficient weight of balls be thrown at the enemy to keep him from charging home. With so many shots fired, many were bound to find targets. A further cogent reason for a close formation was the vulnerability of dispersed infantry to cavalry. The cumbersome loading of the musket gave the foot-soldier no chance of beating off charging horsemen with fire. It, therefore, became necessary to form square and present to the cavalry solid lines of bayonets which could not be outflanked. Squares were normally formed of one or two battalions, and were as often as not oblong rather than square. In case of emergency it was possible for a small body of men to form a 'rallying square', a solid knot of men, which could be built up by newcomers as they arrived.

In the Allied army, between 3,000 and 4,000 men were armed with a rifle. This, a flint-lock piece with a 30-inch barrel containing only a quarter-turn of rifling, was designed by a London gunsmith, Ezekiel Baker. It was accurate up to 300 yards, but was as liable to misfire as the common musket. It was, in addition, a difficult weapon to load, and even an experienced Rifleman could not manage to load and fire in much less than 30 seconds. This was considered to be such a disadvantage that in 1807 Napoleon ordered the withdrawal of all rifles from his army, a fact that put the French in Spain at a permanent disadvantage in skirmishing. Rifles on the Allied side were carried by the 5th battalion of the 60th, by the 95th Rifles, and by a proportion of the men in the two light battalions of the King's German Legion and in the Portuguese *caçadores*.

The normal field-gun in the Anglo-Portuguese artillery was the six-pounder. This could fire either canister or round shot. Canister, a case containing a large number of small balls, was mainly used at very short ranges, 200 or 300 yards. Round (solid) shot was reckoned to be the most effective at ranges up to about 800 yards, although it could be very dangerous after the shot had pitched. 'The plunging of shot', wrote a surgeon, 'usually denominated ricochet is a pleasing although awful and deceitful sight, the ball appearing to bound like a cricket ball; and we are only likely to establish its force by the manner which it ploughs up the ground. A poor Irish lad of the 27th Regiment was silly enough to call out to his comrades on seeing a shot of this kind, "Stop it boys"; and to endeavour to do so with his foot, which was smashed to pieces so as to render amputation necessary.'

Much of the French artillery was of heavier calibre than the Allied, but throughout the war the British had the advantage of Major Shrapnel's recent invention of a shell which burst over the heads of the enemy showering him with musket balls. Another British contribution to the science of artillery, the explosive rocket, developed by Sir William Congreve, gave the Allies some rather erratic assistance in 1813–14.

It is important to remember that all these firearms used black powder, which gave off a considerable quantity of smoke. As a result any close action was fought out in atmospheric conditions not differing greatly from one of London's thicker fogs.

APPENDIX II

Orders of Battle of the Anglo-Portuguese Army

BUSACO

Commander-in-Chief
Lieut.-Gen. Viscount Wellington

Quartermaster-General	*Adjutant-General*
Col. G. Murray	Brig.-Gen. the Hon. Charles Stewart
Commander, Royal Artillery	*Commander, Royal Engineers*
Brig.-Gen. E. Howarth	Col. R. Fletcher

CAVALRY

General Officer Commanding   Maj.-Gen. S. Cotton
4th Dragoons (2 squadrons)

INFANTRY
1st Division
General Officer Commanding   Maj.-Gen. Sir Brent Spencer
1st Brigade (Stopford) 1/Coldstream Gds, 1/3rd Gds., Coy. 5/60th
2nd Brigade (Blantyre) 2/24th, 2/42nd, 1/61st, Coy. 5/60th
3rd Brigade (Loewe) 1st, 2nd, 5th, 7th Line Bns. K.G.L., Dets. Light Bns. K.G.L.
4th Brigade (Pakenham) 1/7th, 1/79th
2nd Division
General Officer Commanding   Lieut.-Gen. R. Hill
1st Brigade (W. Stewart) 1/3rd, 2/31st, 2/48th, 2/66th, Coy. 5/60th
2nd Brigade (Inglis) 29th, 1/48th, 1/57th, Coy. 5/60th
3rd Brigade (Crawford) 2/28th, 2/34th, 2/39th, Coy. 5/60th
3rd Division
General Officer Commanding   Maj.-Gen. T. Picton
1st Brigade (Mackinnon) 1/45th, 74th, 1/88th
2nd Brigade (Lightburne) 2/5th, 2/83rd, 3 Coys. 5/60th
3rd Brigade (Champlemond) 9th and 21st Portuguese Line

4th Division

General Officer Commanding   Maj.-Gen. G. L. Cole
1st Brigade (Alex. Campbell) 2/7th, 1/11th, 2/53rd, Coy. 5/60th
2nd Brigade (Kemmis) 3/27th, 1/40th, 97th, Coy. 5/60th
3rd Brigade (Collins) 11th and 23rd Portuguese Line

5th Division

General Officer Commanding   Maj.-Gen. J. Leith
1st Brigade (Barnes) 3/1st, 1/9th, 2/38th
2nd Brigade (Spry) 3rd and 15th Portuguese Line, 8th Portuguese Line,
   Loyal Lusitanian Legion (3 Bns.).

Light Division

General Officer Commanding   Brig.-Gen. R. Craufurd
1st Brigade (Beckwith) 1/43rd, 1/95th Rifles (4 Coys.), 3rd Caçadores
2nd Brigade (Barclay) 1/52nd, 1/95th Rifles (4 Coys.), 1st Caçadores

Portuguese Division

General Officer Commanding   Maj.-Gen. J. Hamilton
1st Brigade (Archibald Campbell) 4th and 10th Portuguese Line
2nd Brigade (Fonseca) 2nd and 14th Portuguese Line

Independent Brigades

Pack's Brigade: 1st and 16th Portuguese Line, 4th Caçadores
A. Campbell's Brigade: 6th and 18th Portuguese Line, 6th Caçadores
Coleman's Brigade: 7th and 19th Portuguese Line, 2nd Caçadores

SALAMANCA

Commander-in-Chief
General the Earl of Wellington

Quartermaster-General	*Adjutant-General*
Lieut.-Col. W. H. De Lancey (acting)	Lieut.-Col. Lord Aylmer (acting)
Commander, Royal Artillery	*Commander, Royal Engineers*
Lieut.-Col. H. Framingham	Col. R. Fletcher

CAVALRY

General Officer Commanding   Lieut.-Gen. Sir Stapleton Cotton
Le Marchant's Brigade: 5th Dragoon Gds., 3rd and 4th Dragoons
G. Anson's Brigade: 11th, 12th and 16th Light Dragoons
V. von Alten's Brigade: 14th Light Dragoons, 1st Hussars K.G.L.
Bock's Brigade: 1st and 2nd Dragoons K.G.L.
D'Urban's Brigade: 1st and 11th Portuguese Dragoons

INFANTRY
1st Division
General Officer Commanding   Maj.-Gen. H. Campbell (acting)
1st Brigade (Fermor) – as at Busaco
2nd Brigade (Wheatley) 2/24th, 1/42nd, 2/58th, 1/79th, Coy. 5/60th
3rd Brigade (Loewe) 1st, 2nd and 5th Line Bns. K.G.L.
3rd Division
General Officer Commanding   Maj.-Gen. the Hon. Edward Pakenham
1st Brigade (Wallace) 1/45th, 74th, 1/88th, 3 Coys. 5/60th
2nd Brigade (J. Campbell) 1/5th, 2/5th, 2/83rd, 94th
3rd Brigade (Power) 9th and 21st Portuguese Line, 12th Caçadores
4th Division
General Officer Commanding   Maj.-Gen. G. L. Cole
1st Brigade (W. Anson) 3/27th, 1/40th, Coy. 5/60th
2nd Brigade (Ellis) 1/7th, 1/23rd, 1/48th, Coy. Brunswick Oels
3rd Brigade (Stubbs) 11th and 23rd Portuguese Line, 7th Caçadores
5th Division
General Officer Commanding   Lieut.-Gen. J. Leith
1st Brigade (Greville) 3/1st, 1/9th, 1/38th, 2/38th, Coy. Brunswick Oels
2nd Brigade (Pringle) 1/4th, 2/4th, 2/30th, 2/44th, Coy. Brunswick Oels
3rd Brigade (Spry) 3rd and 15th Portuguese Line, 8th Caçadores
6th Division
General Officer Commanding   Maj.-Gen. H. Clinton
1st Brigade (Hulse) 1/11th, 2/53rd, 1/61st, Coy. 5/60th
2nd Brigade (Hinde) 2nd, 1/32nd, 1/36th
3rd Brigade (Rezende) 8th and 12th Portuguese Line, 9th Caçadores
7th Division
General Officer Commanding   Maj.-Gen. J. Hope
1st Brigade (Halket) 1st and 2nd Light Bns. K.G.L., Brunswick Oels (9 Coys.)
2nd Brigade (de Bernewitz) 51st, 68th, Chasseurs Britanniques
3rd Brigade (Collins) 7th and 19th Portuguese Line, 2nd Caçadores
Light Division
General Officer Commanding   Maj.-Gen. Count Charles von Alten
1st Brigade (Barnard) 1/43rd, 2/95th Rifles (4 Coys.), 3/95th Rifles (5 Coys.), 3rd Caçadores
2nd Brigade (Vandeleur) 1/52nd, 1/95th Rifles (8 Coys.), 1st Caçadores
Independent Brigades
Pack's Brigade – as at Busaco
Bradford's Brigade; 13th and 24th Portuguese Line, 5th Caçadores

VITORIA

Commander-in-Chief
General the Marquess of Wellington

Quartermaster-General	*Adjutant-General*
Maj.-Gen. Sir George Murray	Brig.-Gen. Lord Aylmer (acting)
Commander, Royal Artillery	*Commander, Royal Engineers*
Lieut.-Col. A. Dickson	Col. Sir Richard Fletcher, Bt.

CAVALRY

General Officer Commanding Maj.-Gen. E. Bock (acting)

Household Brigade (Robert Hill) 1st and 2nd Life Gds., Royal Horse Gds.

Ponsonby's Brigade: 5th Dragoon Gds.
3rd and 4th Dragoons

Hussar Brigade (Grant) 10th, 15th and 18th Hussars

G. Anson's Brigade: 12th and 16th Light Dragoons

Long's Brigade: 13th Light Dragoons

V. von Alten's Brigade – as at Salamanca

Fane's Brigade: 3rd Dragoon Guards, 1st (Royal) Dragoons

Bock's Brigade: 1st and 2nd Dragoons K.G.L.

D'Urban's Brigade: 1st, 11th, 12th Portuguese Dragoons, 6th Portuguese Dragoons

INFANTRY
1st Division

General Officer Commanding Lieut.-Gen. Sir Thomas Graham

1st Brigade (Stopford) – as at Busaco

2nd Brigade (Halket) 1st, 2nd, 5th Bns. K.G.L., 1st and 2nd Light Bns. K.G.L.

2nd Division

General Officer Commanding Lieut.-Gen. Sir Rowland Hill

1st Brigade (Cadogan) 1/50th, 1/71st, 1/92nd, Coy. 5/60th

2nd Brigade (Byng) 1/3rd, 1/57th, 1st Provisional Bn. (2/31st and 2/66th)

3rd Brigade (O'Callaghan) 1/28th, 2/34th, 1/39th, Coy. 5/60th

4th Brigade (Ashworth) 6th and 18th Portuguese Line, 6th Caçadores

3rd Division

General Officer Commanding Lieut.-Gen. Sir Thomas Picton

1st Brigade (Brisbane) – as at Salamanca

2nd Brigade (Colville) 1/5th, 2/83rd, 2/87th, 94th

3rd Brigade (Power) – as at Salamanca

4th Division

General Officer Commanding   Lieut.-Gen. Sir Lowry Cole

1st Brigade (W. Anson) 3/27th, 1/40th, I/48th, 2nd Provisional Bn. (2nd and 2/53rd) Coy. 5/60th

2nd Brigade (Skerret) 1/7th, 20th, 1/23rd, Coy. Brunswick Oels

3rd Brigade (Stubbs) — as at Salamanca

5th Division

General Officer Commanding   Maj.-Gen. Oswald (acting)

1st Brigade (Hay) 3/1st, 1/9th, 1/38th, Coy. Brunswick Oels

2nd Brigade (Robinson) 1/4th, 2/47th, 2/59th, Coy. Brunswick Oels

3rd Brigade (Spry) — as at Salamanca

7th Division

General Officer Commanding   Lieut.-Gen. the Earl of Dalhousie

1st Brigade (Barnes) 1/6th, 3rd Provisional Bn. (2/24th and 2/58th), Brunswick Oels (9 Coys.)

2nd Brigade (Grant) 51st, 68th, 1/82nd, Chasseurs Britanniques

3rd Brigade (Le Cor) — as at Salamanca

Light Division

General Officer Commanding   Maj.-Gen. Count Charles von Alten

1st Brigade (Kempt) 1/43rd, 1/95th Rifles (8 Coys.), 3/95th Rifles (5 Coys.), 3rd Caçadores

2nd Brigade (Vandeleur) 1/52nd, 2/95th Rifles (6 Coys.), 17th Portuguese Line, 1st Caçadores

Portuguese Division

General Officer Commanding   Maj.-Gen. Conde de Amaranthe

1st Brigade (A. Campbell) 4th and 10th Portuguese Line, 10th Caçadores

2nd Brigade (Da Costa) — as at Busaco

Independent Brigades

Pack's Brigade — as at Busaco

Bradford's Brigade — as at Salamanca

NIVELLE

Commander-in-Chief

Field-Marshal the Marquess of Wellington

Quartermaster-General	*Adjutant-General*
Maj.-Gen. Sir George Murray	Maj.-Gen. the Hon. Edward Pakenham
Commander, Royal Artillery	*Commander, Royal Engineers*
Lieut.-Col. A. Dickson	Lieut.-Col. H. Elphinstone

CAVALRY

General Officer Commanding   Lieut.-Gen. Sir Stapleton Cotton

V. von Alten's Brigade: 18th Hussars, 1st Hussars K.G.L.

Grant's Brigade: 13th and 14th Light Dragoons

INFANTRY

1st Division

General Officer Commanding   Lieut.-Gen. Sir John Hope

Maj.-Gen. Howard (acting)

1st Brigade (Stopford) — as at Busaco

2nd Brigade (Maitland) 1/1st Guards, 3/1st Guards, Coy. 5/60th

3rd Brigade (Hinüber) — as at Vitoria

2nd Division

General Officer Commanding   Lieut.-Gen. Sir Rowland Hill

Lieut.-Gen. the Hon. William Stewart (acting)

1st Brigade (Walker) — as at Vitoria

2nd Brigade (Byng) — as at Vitoria

3rd Brigade (Pringle) — as at Vitoria

4th Brigade (Ashworth) — as at Vitoria

3rd Division

General Officer Commanding   Maj.-Gen. the Hon. Charles Colville (acting)

1st Brigade (Brisbane) — as at Salamanca

2nd Brigade (Keane) — as at Vitoria

3rd Brigade (Power) — as at Salamanca

4th Division

General Officer Commanding   Lieut.-Gen. Sir Lowry Cole

1st Brigade (W. Anson) — as at Vitoria

2nd Brigade (Ross) — as at Vitoria

3rd Brigade (Vasconcello) — as at Salamanca

5th Division

General Officer Commanding   Maj.-Gen. A. Hay (acting)

1st Brigade (Greville) 3/1st, 1/9th, 1/38th, 2/47th, Coy. Brunswick Oels

2nd Brigade (Robinson) 1/4th, 2/59th, 2/84th, Coy. Brunswick Oels

3rd Brigade (De Regoa) — as at Salamanca

6th Division

General Officer Commanding   Lieut.-Gen. Sir Henry Clinton

1st Brigade (Pack) 1/42nd, 1/79th, 1/91st, Coy. 5/60th

2nd Brigade (Lambert) 1/11th, 1/32nd, 1/61st

3rd Brigade (Douglas) — as at Salamanca

7th Division

General Officer Commanding   Maj.-Gen. Le Cor

1st Brigade (Barnes) – as at Vitoria

2nd Brigade (Inglis) – as at Vitoria

3rd Brigade (Doyle) – as at Salamanca

Light Division

General Officer Commanding   Maj.-Gen. Count Charles von Alten

1st Brigade (Kempt) – as at Vitoria

2nd Brigade (Colborne) – as at Vitoria

Portuguese Division

General Officer Commanding   Lieut.-Gen. Sir James Hamilton

1st Brigade (Buchan) – as at Busaco

2nd Brigade (Da Costa) – as at Busaco

Independent Brigades

Wilson's Brigade – as Pack's at Busaco

Bradford's Brigade – as at Salamanca

Aylmer's Brigade: 2/62nd, 76th, 77th, 85th

Bibliography

ASPINALL-OGLANDER, C.,★ *Freshly Remembered*, 1956
BARNARD, A., *The Barnard Letters* (ed. A. Powell), 1928
BATTY, R., *Campaign in the Western Pyrenees and South of France*, 1823
BEAMISH, N. L.,★ *History of the King' s German Legion*, 1832
BEATSON, F. C.,★ *With Wellington in the Pyrenees*, 1914
   The Bidassoa and Nivelle, 1931
BELL, G., *Rough Notes of an Old Soldier*, 1867
BLAKENEY, R., *A Boy in the Peninsular War* (ed. J. Sturgis), 1899
BLAKISTON, J., *Twelve Years' Military Adventure*, 1829
BRETT-JAMES, A.,★ *General Graham, Lord Lynedoch*, 1959
BUNBURY, K., *Reminiscences of a Veteran*, 1861
BURGOYNE, J., *Life and Correspondence* (ed. G. Wrottesley), 1873
CHAMBERS, G.,★ *Bussaco*, 1910
COLBORNE, J., *Life of John Colborne, Lord Seaton* (ed. G. C. Moore Smith), 1903
COLE, G. L., *Memoirs of Sir Lowry Cole* (ed. M. L. Cole and S. Gwynn), 1934
COOK, J. H., *Memoir of the Late War*, 1831
   Narrative of Events in the South of France, 1835
COOPER, J. Spencer, *Rough Notes of Seven Campaigns*, 1869
COPE, W. H.,★ *History of the Rifle Brigade*, 1877
COSTELLO, E., *The Adventures of a Soldier*, 1841
CRAUFURD, A. H.,★ *General Craufurd and His Light Division*, 1892
CROKER, J. W.,★ *The Croker Papers* (ed. L. W. Jennings), 1884
DAVIES, G.,★ *Wellington and His Army*, 1954
DICKSON, A., *The Dickson Manuscripts, Series C.* (ed. J. H. Leslie), 1908–12
DONALDSON, J., *Recollections of the Eventful Life of a Soldier*, 1825
D'URBAN, B., *Peninsular Journal* (ed. I. J. Rousseau), 1930
FORTESCUE, J.,★ *History of the British Army*, vols. vi–x, 1919–20
FOY, M., *Vie Militaire de Général Foy* (ed. M. Girod de l'Ain), 1900
FRAZER, A. S., *Letters of Sir A. S. Frazer* (ed. E. Sabine), 1859
FREER, W. & E., *Letters from the Peninsula* (ed. N. Scarfe), 1953
GAVIN, W., 'Diary of William Gavin, 1806–1815' (ed. C. Oman), *H. L. I. Journal*, 1920–21
GOMM, W., *Letters and Journals* (ed. F. C. Carr-Gomm), 1881
GRONOW, R. H., *Reminiscences of Captain Grownow*, 1862
HALL, F., 'Peninsular Recollections, 1811–1812', *R.U.S.I. Journal*, 1912–13
HAY, A. Leith, *A Narrative of the Peninsular War*, 1834
HAY, W., *Reminiscences under Wellington* (ed. Mrs. S. C. I. Wood), 1901
HENRY, W., *Events of a Military Life*, 1843
JONES, J. T., *Account of the War in Spain, Portugal and the South of France*, 1821
   Journal of the Sieges in Spain, 1827
JOURDAN, J.-B., *Mémoires Militaires*, 1899

★ Indicates that the author was not present in the Peninsula

KENNEDY, J. Shaw, *Diary 1810*, published with Fitzclarence, *Manual of Outpost Duties*, 1849

KINCAID, J. *Adventures in the Rifle Brigade*, 1830
Random Shots from a Rifleman, 1835

LARPENT, F. S., *Private Journal*, 1852

LEACH, J., *Rough Sketches of the Life of an Old Soldier*, 1831

L'ESTRANGE, G. B., *Recollections*, 1874

LEVINGE, R.,★ *Historical Records of the 43rd Light Infantry*, 1868

LEWIN, H. Ross, *With the Thirty-Second in the Peninsula* (ed. J. Wardell), 1914

LONG, R. B. *Peninsular Cavalry General* (ed. T. H. McGuffie), 1951

MACCARTHY, J., *Recollections of the Storming of the Castle of Badajoz*, 1836

MCGRIGOR, J., *Autobiography and Services*, 1861

MAXWELL, W. H. (ed.),★ *Peninsular Sketches*, 1845

MOORE, J., *Diary of Sir John Moore* (ed. J. F. Maurice), 1904

MORLEY, S., *Memoirs of a Serjeant of the 5th Regiment of Foot*, 1842

MOORSOM, W. S.,★ *Historical Records of the 52nd Regiment*, 1860

MUNSTER, Earl of, *Account of the British Campaign of 1809 in Portugal and Spain*, 1831

NAPIER, G., *Passages in the Early Military Life of Sir George T. Napier*, 1884

NAPIER, W., *History of the Peninsular War* (Cabinet Edition), 1853
Life of Sir William Napier (ed. H. A. Bruce), 1864

OMAN, C,★ *History of the Peninsular War*, 1902–30
Wellington's Army, 1913

PATTERSON, J., *Adventures of Captain John Patterson*, 1837

ROBINSON, H. B.,★ *Memoirs of Lt.-Gen. Sir Thomas Picton*, 1835

SCHAUMANN, A. E. F., *On the Road with Wellington* (trans. A. M. Ludovici), 1924

SHERER, G. M., *Recollections of the Peninsula*, 1823

SIDNEY, E.,★ *Life of Lord Hill*, 1845

SIMMONS, G., *A British Rifleman* (ed. W. Verner), 1899

SMITH, H., *Autobiography* (ed. G. C. Moore Smith), 1901

STANHOPE, Earl of,★ *Conversations with the Duke of Wellington*, 1881

STAVELY, W., 'One of Wellington's Staff Officers' (ed. L. Jackson), *Journal of the Society for Army Historical Research*, Autumn 1935

SURTEES, W., *Twenty-five Years in the Rifle Brigade*, 1833

SYNGE, Charles, 'Captain Synge's Experiences at Salamanca', *The Nineteenth Century*, July 1912

TOMKINSON, W., *Diary of a Cavalry Officer* (ed. J. Tomkinson), 1894

VERE, C. Broke, *Marches, Movements and Operations of the Fourth Division*, 1841

VERNER, W.,★ *History and Campaigns of the Rifle Brigade*, 1912–19

WARD, S. G. P.,★ *Wellington's Headquarters*, 1957

WARRE, W., *Letters from the Peninsula* (ed. E. Warre), 1909

WELLINGTON, Duke of, *Despatches* (ed. J. Gurwood), 1834–1839
Despatches, Correspondence and Memoranda (ed. 2nd Duke of Wellington), 1858–72

WHEELER, W., *Letters of Private Wheeler* (ed. B. H. Liddell Hart), 1951

WHINYATES, E. C., Letters in *The Whinyates Family Record* (ed. F. T. Whinyates), 1894–96

WOOD, G., *The Subaltern Officer*, 1825

ANON., *Journal of a Soldier of the 71st or Glasgow Regiment*, 1828

ANON., *Memoirs of a Serjeant, late in the 43rd Light Infantry Regiment*, 1835

ANON., *Letters from Portugal, Spain and France during the Memorable Campaigns of 1811, 1812, and 1813*, 1819

Index